Conserving, Preserving, and Restoring Your Heritage

GENEALOGIST'S REFERENCE SHELF

Conserving, Preserving, and Restoring Your Heritage

KENNIS KIM

DUNDURN PRESS
TORONTO

Editor: Ruth Chernia
Proofreader: Nicole Chaplin
Designer: Jennifer Scott
Printer: Transcontinental

Library and Archives Canada Cataloguing in Publication

Kim, Kennis
Conserving, preserving, and restoring your heritage : a professional's advice / by Kennis Kim.

Co-published by the Ontario Genealogical Society.
Includes bibliographical references.
ISBN 978-1-55488-462-9

1. Material culture--Conservation and restoration. 2. Antiquities--Collection and preservation. I. Ontario Genealogical Society II. Title.

AM313.K54 2010 702.8'8 C2009-907211-4

1 2 3 4 5 14 13 12 11 10

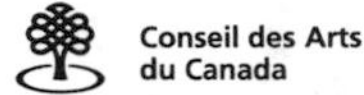

Canada Council for the Arts
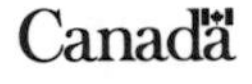

We acknowledge the support of the **Canada Council for the Arts** and the **Ontario Arts Council** for our publishing program. We also acknowledge the financial support of the **Government of Canada** through the **Book Publishing Industry Development Program** and **The Association for the Export of Canadian Books**, and the **Government of Ontario** through the **Ontario Book Publishers Tax Credit program**, and the **Ontario Media Development Corporation**.

Care has been taken to trace the ownership of copyright material used in this book. The author and the publisher welcome any information enabling them to rectify any references or credits in subsequent editions.

J. Kirk Howard, President

Printed and bound in Canada.
www.dundurn.com

Ontario Genealogical Society
Suite 102, 40 Orchard View Boulevard
Toronto, Ontario, Canada M4R 1B9
tel. (416) 489-0734 fax. (416) 489-9803
provoffice@ogs.on.ca *www.ogs.on.ca*

Dundurn Press
3 Church Street, Suite 500
Toronto, Ontario, Canada
M5E 1M2

Gazelle Book Services Limited
White Cross Mills
High Town, Lancaster, England
LA1 4XS

Dundurn Press
2250 Military Road
Tonawanda, NY
U.S.A. 14150

CONTENTS

Appendices

INTRODUCTION

History surrounds us — in museums, in our communities, and in our homes. Whether objects were bought, found, or inherited, these artifacts offer glimpses into the past — a time, place, event, or person we wish to remember and share with the future.

As custodians of pieces of our history, we are faced with how to maintain these items. Our family history may be held in documents, photographs, books, clothing, or textiles, and sometimes complete collections of items such as coins, trading cards, or stamps. We may have little knowledge of the artifacts we hold except that they meant something to someone, and now we feel an obligation or desire to preserve them for future generations. How we choose to execute our stewardship over these items takes many forms depending on their use, importance, and condition. More importantly, how we care for the items may be determined by what we know and what we can do financially without causing additional damage and deterioration. This book will guide you through some basic preservation techniques and preventative **conservation** practices for artifacts commonly found in family collections.

Many new terms are introduced through the text to help give you a better understanding of preservation, conservation, and restoration of your family heirlooms. All of the terms in bold can be found in the glossary.

There are many resources to help with the initial sorting and evaluation of historic documents and artifacts, including *Help! I've Inherited an Attic Full of History* by Althea Douglas, published by the Ontario Genealogical Society in 2003. Once you've determined what you have, it's time to decide how you'll care for these things. Before you do anything, you should document what you have both in a written format and photographically, if possible. An **accession list** of all your holdings, will help you to know what you have and where it is, and help you decide what you might do with it. An accession list, similar to an inventory, can be made using an index card for each item or in a list on paper or in your computer. Whatever method of compiling the information you use, always keep a hard copy in a safe place somewhere other than your home. Having an accession list and photographs of your items can be helpful in recovering stolen goods, filing insurance claims, and sharing information, images, or documents with others without jeopardizing the originals.

A basic accession list can be as simple as listing the items either in groups or individually. Include what it is, where it came from, and where it's located in your home (see Appendix 1: Accession List Information). Additional information might include condition notes, value, if it's insured, historic significance, supporting research, conservation reports, and any other information that may relate to the artifact. Photographs can be slides, prints, or digital files.

The decision to display, store, or continue to use an artifact should in part be based on the condition and structural stability of the object. If an item is stable and in good condition, you can prepare it at home for display or storage. However, if an item is damaged or fragile, it may be necessary to call a professional (see Appendix 2: How to Find and Choose a Conservation Professional). Choose the right professional for your artifacts by considering the type of items, their overall condition, and the intended use of the objects. Storage, use, display, or just ignoring things all have consequences.

CHAPTER I

The Home Environment

What are conservation, restoration, and preservation?

Conservation is the examination, stabilization, reconstruction (restoration), and reduction of further deterioration (preservation) of an object. Conservation often includes:

- Scientific analysis of the object and the materials used during fabrication,
- Research into the structure and historic significance of an artifact, and
- Determination of overall condition and stability of the artifact.

Restoration refers to the reconstruction of the aesthetic appearance of an object. This is a small part of the conservation process.

Preservation is another small part of the conservation process that focuses on treatments to retard further deterioration of an object.

The most we are able to do in our homes are preservation and some basic preventative conservation. To preserve the structural stability and to slow deterioration of objects, you must pay attention to the environment, including light, temperature, and **relative humidity**, as well as the methods of handling, displaying, and storing the object.

Environmental Concerns

Light

All light is a form of energy. When light energy is absorbed by an artifact, it causes chemical changes in the molecular structure of the object. Natural and artificial light can damage objects by fading colours, yellowing varnishes, bleaching paper, and weakening textiles.

For our purposes, the light spectrum can be divided into three parts: infrared, ultraviolet, and visible light. Visible light is the part of the range of light between the ultraviolet and infrared parts of the light spectrum. Ultraviolet (UV) light is invisible. UV light falls beyond the blue portion of visible light. Infrared (IR) is also invisible. It falls just past the red portion of visible light.

Light is measured in **foot-candles**, **lumens**, or **lux**. You can determine an approximation of the number of lux at home using a single lens reflex (SLR) camera or a light meter (see Appendix 3: Using a Camera to Measure Approximate Light Levels).

Ultraviolet light is the most energetic form of light radiation and causes the most damage. To reduce UV damage, it is important to reduce UV exposure. You can do this in three ways:

1. Always use low-UV emitting light sources, such as incandescent bulbs. Tungsten-halogen lamps and fluorescent lamps (both traditional fluorescent tubes and the new energy-saving spiral bulbs) have higher UV output than incandescent bulbs but lower UV than natural daylight.
2. There are UV filters that block the UV from light sources such as fluorescent bulbs and on windows. UV filters come in the form of sleeves that slip over fluorescent tubes and films that can be applied to glass or windows. There are also plastics and glass for framing and display of artifacts with UV reducers incorporated into their structure.
3. Bouncing light off a painted surface will reduce much of the damaging UV energy in natural light.

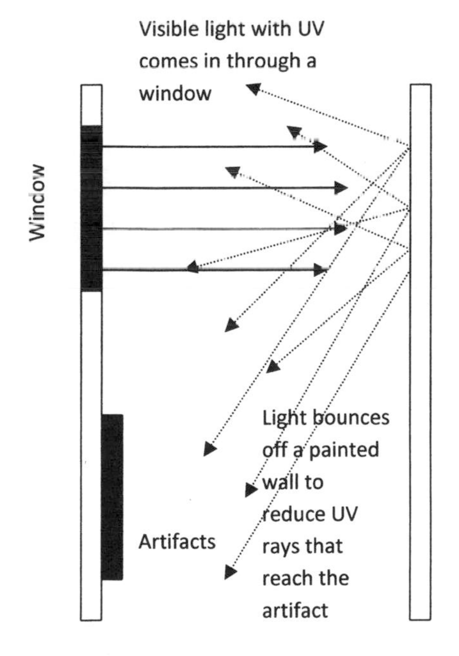

Diagram 1:
Reflecting light — a method of reducing the damage from UV sources

Infrared light (IR) is less damaging than UV because it has less energy, but it is more easily absorbed by the surface of an object. IR may be thought of as heat because it causes an object to warm up, which speeds chemical deterioration. Dark surfaces absorb heat more readily than light surfaces. To reduce heat build-up, avoid direct sunlight and move incandescent bulbs away from artifacts.

Visible light falls between the UV and IR portions of the light spectrum. Light that appears blue is closer to the UV end of the spectrum and is more damaging to artifacts. Examples of blue light sources are cool fluorescent lamps, full-spectrum fluorescent lamps, and sunlight. Warm fluorescent lamps have lower amounts of blue light and incandescent lamps have the lowest amount of blue light. UV filtered sunlight is far more damaging than the visible light emitted from an incandescent lamp. Never use picture lights mounted onto a frame; they are too close to the artifact's surface. Never use direct spotlights that are closer than three metres to the artifact.

To reduce damage from visible light, you should reduce the amount of daylight and glare from glossy surfaces to produce lower light levels acceptable for viewing. This can be achieved by indirect lighting: either reflecting light off another surface or lighting from an angle. Light damage is cumulative and depends on the intensity of the light level as well as the length of exposure. Rotate light sensitive items that are displayed so that artifacts will have time to "rest" in dark storage.

Temperature

Heat, cold, and cycling of temperatures cause damage to artifacts. When an artifact is warmed, the rate of chemical reactions within the molecular structure increases. These reactions are the deterioration of the artifact. Ambient temperature and exposure to IR light sources such as daylight, incandescent lamps, or spotlights cause warming of an object. Darker objects absorb more energy and warm quicker than lighter surfaces. If an object heats, cools, or cycles through rapid changes of temperature of more than 10 degrees within a short period of time (one to two hours), the result can be significant dimensional change: expansion and contraction.

Relative Humidity

Relative humidity (RH) is a percentage representing the amount of water vapour in the air compared to the total amount of water the air can hold at that temperature. A relative humidity of 100 percent at a given temperature would refer to complete saturation of the air by the water vapour present.

Changes in the RH do not greatly affect most people's comfort level but a temperature change of a few degrees does make a difference in how comfortable you feel. Art and artifacts react much more to changes in RH than shifts in temperature. It is much more important to stabilize the RH levels than the temperature for the stability and long-term care of objects.

Damage seen at RH 70 percent and above:

- micro-organisms: **mould** and **mildew**
- deformations from plane as a result of tension loss

Damage seen at less than 35 percent RH:

- shrinking
- warping

- cracking
- drying out of adhesives
- desiccation

Cycles of RH with changes of more than 5 percent an hour result in expansion and contraction that lead to:

- cracking
- warping
- splitting
- water staining due to condensation
- separation of component layers
- deformations from plane (when an artifact undulates, warps, twists, or distorts causing it no longer to be flat or in its intended shape)

The environment plays an important role in the overall stability and preservation of an artifact. Unfortunately, much structural damage is a result of infestations, poor handling, and human error (see Appendix 4: General Rules for Handling and Moving Artifacts and Works of Art).

Insects and Rodents

Insects

The most common insects found in home collections are the book-lice or paper lice, cockroach, silverfish, firebrats, moths, and carpet and cigarette beetles. It is always best to try and prevent an infestation rather than have to control one, but insects are a common problem. Whenever possible, attempt to use deterrents and mechanical means of controlling an infestation before applying chemicals that could potentially be harmful to the artifacts or humans.

Book-lice (*Liposcelidoe*) are also known as paper lice. This almost microscopic insect normally lives outdoors feeding on microscopic moulds growing in damp situations. They have no wings but can enter buildings carried on papers, furniture, or boxes that may also be supporting mould growth. Once introduced, book-lice become numerous, especially in the late summer when both the temperature and relative humidity are high. In addition to feeding on mould, they feed on the adhesives in books and wallpaper, as well as cereals and paper products, but do not seem to cause holes as with silverfish and roaches. They are transparent to grey in colour.

Control of an infestation is difficult since book-lice are numerous and easily reintroduced to a collection. Book-lice do not need males for reproduction and can produce up to eight generations a year. Twenty to 90 eggs are laid and hatch in 6 to 21 days. Reduction of humidity will reduce the presence of book-lice.

Cockroaches belong to the insect order *Blattaria*. Roaches are primarily nocturnal. They breed throughout the year. Eggs are laid in batches of 18 to 50 per capsule and are carried by the female until close to hatching time, about 14 to 30 days. Roaches are able to squeeze through very narrow openings and are good climbers. They feed on books, paper, bindings, adhesives, and any other starchy products. Damage from feeding appears as holes or notches. In addition to the damage caused by chewing, roaches cause a great deal of staining as a result of vomiting, depositing feces, secreting fluid from their abdominal glands, or adhesion of egg casings.

Control of a roach infestation is best done by improved sanitation, minimizing water and condensation, and discarding excess paper and cardboard. When storing artifacts, change wooden storage furniture to stainless steel and, as a deterrent, place paper products in plastic containers rather than paper or cardboard.

If roach infestations recur, you may need to take additional measures. Replace hollow doors with solid core, install insect-proof outlets, store all food products in plastic containers, and seal access between rooms and floors (such as via plumbing and electrical wiring). Non-chemical sticky traps placed directly against the wall near water sources can control an infestation, but fumigation, insecticides, or baits may be required.

Silverfish (*Lepisma saccharina*) and firebrats (*Themobia domestica*) have very similar characteristics and feeding habits. The primary difference is that silverfish prefer cool damp conditions and firebrats like hot and humid conditions. The silverfish lays about 100 eggs singly or in groups of twos or threes. Firebrats lay about 50. Adults of both may live two years or longer. Both insects eat carbohydrate and protein-rich foods including fabrics, papers, and adhesives. They particularly like the **sizing** applied to paper and fabrics during processing. Common evidence of damage includes holes and notches as well as what appears to be scraped or thinned paper.

You can control an infestation mechanically by lowering the ambient temperature. If possible, freezing will kill firebrat nymphs. Using plastic storage containers, reducing the humidity, and increasing light will deter these insects. You may need to use sticky traps, fumigants, or insecticides.

Carpet beetles (several species) and cigarette beetles (*Lasioderma serricorne F*) are serious threats to books and textiles. It is the beetles' larvae that cause the most damage to collections as they feed on upholstery, stuffing, dried flowers, fabric, wood, paper, and adhesives.

Dry cleaning or vacuuming infested fabrics, furniture, and books can help control an insect problem. Freezing for 72 hours is a proven method of killing some beetles. Capture a specimen to determine a course of action. Chemical extermination may be required.

The most common clothes moths are the case making moth (*Tinea pellionella Linnaeus*) and the web making moth (*Tineola bisselliella Hummel*). Web making moths lay eggs singly or in small groups within the fibres of the infested material. The eggs are secured to the infested material with a gelatinous excretion. The emerging larvae spin webs consisting of fibres from the infested support and feces. The webbing, often in a tubular form, spreads as the larvae travel across the fabric.

Case making moths have habits similar to the web making moths except that the larva spins a case of silk that is interwoven with fibres removed from the support during feeding, but the case is not attached to the support material. The larvae drag their cases with them and will die if the case is removed.

Vacuuming, freezing, and cleaning are all methods to control moth infestations without fumigants (see Appendix 11: Treating Infestations in Textiles by Freezing).

There are many other insects and rodents that will attack collections. If an infestation is suspected, it is best to try to capture a sample of the pest to determine the most appropriate methods of controlling the infestation.

Rodents

During spring and fall, it is quite common for rodents such as mice, rats, and squirrels to try and find a way into your home. Raccoons and opossums like to find winter refuge in attics, garages, and other outdoor storage structures. Rodents destroy and damage artifacts by feeding on them or using paper and fabrics, especially furniture stuffing, as nesting materials.

Once a rodent has found its way into a space, it tends to return repeatedly. If young are born, they too can return seasonally unless entry is prevented. It is best to store your artifacts within your living space where infestations are less likely to happen and, if rodents do enter, the infestation will be discovered quickly.

CHAPTER 2

Paper, Parchment, and Vellum

Most manuscripts, legal documents, public records, diplomas, drawings, and many other two-dimensional artifacts are created on **paper**, **parchment**, or **vellum**. Paper is produced from the pulp of wood; parchment and vellum are made from the un-tanned skin of animals. In the Middle Ages, the term vellum was used to describe fine parchment. Vellum was sometimes dyed a rich purple for very important documents.

Preservation Concerns

The preservation concerns for most two-dimensional works can be divided into:

1. Issues with the **support**, such as the paper or parchment.
2. Problems with whatever **medium** was applied to the support, such as ink, charcoal, or pencil.

Paper supports are very prone to **acid** deterioration. Paper is made from **cellulose** extracted from wood pulp by strong chemicals. The paper produced contains acids left over from the pulping process. Additional acids build up in paper as the **lignin** in the pulp deteriorates with age, and with exposure to the sulphuric acid that is produced when the moisture in the air contacts sulphur dioxide from coal and petroleum combustion. Art and documents discolour and become brittle as these acids cause deterioration of the molecular structure.

Parchment and other hides are naturally very strong and can withstand a great deal of manipulation due to their composition. During the preparation of hides, **alkaline** substances are applied making the sheets resistant to acid deterioration. The greatest preservation issues relate to their extreme sensitivity to moisture. Hides often illustrate varying degrees of **buckling** and **deformations** due to changes in the relative humidity. This buckling can be so severe that it interferes with the aesthetics of the piece.

Paper, too, can buckle or become deformed due to changes in relative humidity, but the more troublesome risk of exposing paper to high humidity is **foxing**. Foxing refers to small brown spots that form on paper that can be visually disturbing and result in small holes. It is thought that foxing is a mould growth as a result of impurities in the structure of the paper or the sizing material that was applied to the paper during production.

An exposure to water or 68–70 percent RH will allow mould to attack the sizing applied to the paper, the medium, or the structure of the paper (cellulose), parchment, or vellum. Mould is a health hazard and it disfigures and visually alters artifacts.

Other problems common to paper and parchment supports include discolouration, yellowing, darkening from light exposure, fading, or colour change due to light exposure, darkening due to exposure to acidic materials, matt burn, liquid staining, oil

Table 1:
Environmental Recommendations for Paper-Based Artifacts

Type of Object	Recommended Relative Humidity	Recommended Temperatures	Recommended Light Levels
Book Bindings	45– 60% Above 65% promotes mould growth	18°–20°C (65-68°F) never above 25°C	50–150 lux
Paper	40–50%	8–21°C (60–70°F)	50–100 lux
Parchment or Vellum	45–55% > 65% intake of moisture increased rapidly 68–70% promotes mould growth	18–21°C (60–70°F)	50–100 lux
Photographic Materials	30–45%	18–20°C (65–68°F)	50–100 lux colour photos 100-200 lux black-and-white

staining (frequently from fingerprints), media-induced staining, adhesive staining, adhesive residue, creases, folds, tears, holes, surface abrasion and fibre loss, pinholes, flyspecks (which appear as dark irregular dots), insect damage, attachment to inadequate or damaging support materials, applied adhesive, or damage as a result of previous inappropriate repairs.

The **media** used to produce documents and works of art on paper can be just as prone to deterioration as the paper supporting them. Although graphite and pencil are relatively stable, pastels, charcoal, and chalk are all powdery and smudge easily. There are commercially available fixatives, but they should probably be avoided as they can change the colour of the pigments and trap dirt on the surface; some have been linked to deterioration of the paper supports. It is common for twentieth-century blue and black inks of fountain, ballpoint, and felt-tipped pens to fade to a brown colour because the inks were made from dyes rather than pigments. Some of these inks are so unstable they even fade when in dark storage. Older inks also have problems, especially early twentieth-century iron-gall ink. The gallic acid reacts with the iron resulting in corrosion that destroys the paper on which the ink was written. This appears like burns and holes in the paper.

Tempera and other paints applied to a sheet of paper or parchment can begin to flake or powder, resulting in losses from the image layer on the support. When the support, whether paper or parchment, is not handled properly when moved, it flexes and bends causing the more rigid applied media to flake off. Movement in the form of small expansions and contractions also occur when there are changes in the relative humidity. This too results in losses of the applied media.

Specific rules for handling various artifacts are given in Appendix 4: General Rules for Handling and Moving Artifacts and Works of Art, but here are some general guidelines to remember:

- Try not to directly touch the artifacts. The oils occurring naturally on your skin can damage and stain your treasures.
- Handle items with **mount** and **matt** boards by the supporting board.
- Handling un-mounted sheets by lifting them by the upper corners so that they hang freely without bending.
- Wear gloves when working with artifacts. White cotton gloves are recommended.
- Always place artifacts on a clean and level surface.

Preventative Conservation

The first step in preservation is to always thoroughly examine your artifact for damage and potential problems and check the overall structural stability of the work. One of the most common and helpful things that can be done at home is a very light, dry surface cleaning to reduce the amount of dust, fibres, and other foreign material that may have collected on the surface. *Never* attempt to clean brittle papers or powdery media, such as pastels, chalk, charcoal, or painted surfaces.

Surface dirt should be removed not only to improve the aesthetic appearance of the piece but also to eliminate a hazard. Dirt is abrasive, it can be acidic, and it holds moisture, which promotes the growth of mould spores. If your work can tolerate a light cleaning, you will need a very soft natural bristled brush, an **air bulb** (either the type used for a baby's nose or those sold at photographic supply stores), and a **drafting brush**.

Wearing white cotton gloves, you should begin by gently blowing away any loose surface dirt with the air bulb. Follow this by brushing lightly with the soft natural bristled brush. Begin brushing from the centre of the object and work toward the edges. Use very light pressure; the paper should not move with your brush strokes. As dirt and dust accumulate around the edge of your artifact and on your work surface, remove it using the drafting brush. Once the surface dirt has been reduced, the artifact can be prepared for storage or display.

Storage and Display

Where items will be stored is as important as the method and materials for storage. Roofs leak, basements flood, and the temperature in attics fluctuates greatly day to night and through the seasons. Careful consideration should be given to the type of artifact to be stored and the conditions of storage. In bad conditions, deterioration can happen rapidly and with heart-breaking consequences.

Once you have determined a location for storage, chose the storage method and materials. Print files or drawers available from office, art, and drafting suppliers are very space efficient. Metal files with a baked-on finish are preferable to wood because wood is acidic and acid contamination can be transferred to your stored artifacts, resulting in damage.

Solander boxes or storage boxes made from **acid-free** corrugated board, acid-free and lignin-free box boards (TrueCore), or corrugated copolymer (**Coroplast**) can be arranged within the metal file drawers to help organize your holdings by size, subject, or medium. Ideally, artifacts should be matted prior to storage, but this is very costly.

When stacking matted, mounted, or loose artifacts, place separation sheets between each work. There are many materials that can be used to separate the artifacts: **glassine**, interleafing tissue, **Permalife** paper, **Melinex** (clear **polyester** film), or PermaDur to name a few. Each has advantages and disadvantages and you should research which is best for your collection. Table 2: Papers and Characteristics offers a limited comparison of some of the archival papers available. Folders made of acid-free stock are another alternative for sorting your collection and separating works within file drawers or boxes.

Damaged items can be protected by placing the items in a folder or an envelope or by encapsulating the artifact between two sheets of clear polyester film (Melinex — see Appendix 5: Encapsulation Process). Do *not* confuse encapsulation in polyester film with lamination. Lamination is an irreversible process

Table 2:
Papers and Characteristics

Papers and Characteristics	Permalife	Melinex	Buffered Interleafing Tissue	Unbuffered Interleafing Tissue	Glassine	Standard Barrier Interleafing Paper — Buffered	PermaDur Buffered and Unbuffered Paper
Buffered	Yes, pH 7.5–8.0	Inert	Yes	No	No, pH 6 8–7.0	Yes	Available buffered
Acid-free	Yes, pH 8.0–8.5, Lignin-free	Inert — acts as barrier against acid transfer	Yes	As it ages it absorbs acid and becomes acidic	Yes	Yes	Yes, Unbuffered paper becomes acidic as it ages and absorbs acid
Transparency	No	Transparent	(.001) thickness is translucent	(.001) thickness is translucent	Semi-transparent	No	No
Static	No	Yes — not to be used with loose media (chalk, pastel, etc.)	No	No	No static — very smooth surface	No	No
Format	Sheets and rolls	Rolls, sheets, pre-made enclosures	Rolls or sheets	Rolls or sheets	Rolls or sheets	Rolls	Sheets

Continued on following page

Table 2:
Papers and Characteristics

Papers and Characteristics	Permalife	Melinex	Buffered Interleafing Tissue	Unbuffered Interleafing Tissue	Glassine	Standard Barrier Interleafing Paper — Buffered	PermaDur Buffered and Unbuffered Paper
Use with	Make high quality copies, line boxes, interleaf	Documents	Phtography — silver halide films or papers, and nitrate films; Cotton fabrics, paper	Colour prints, wool or silk textiles, watercolours, drawings, lithographs, parchment	Newspapers, magazines, watercolours, and drawings	Frame backing, documents, prints	Making folders
Not recommended	Animal products: parchment, wool, vellum, silk, or leather	Pastels, chalk, textiles, any loose or flaking material	Animal products: parchment, wool, vellum, silk, or leather	General purpose	Not for photographs	Animal products: parchment, wool, vellum, silk, or leather	Do not use buffered paper with animal products: parchment, wool, vellum, silk or leather
Approximate Cost 2008*	From $17.79 per 500 sheets	From $17.00 per 25 sheets	From $6.00 per 100 sheets	From $5.50 per 100 sheets	From $4.50 per 100 sheets	From $0.13 per yard sold as 250 yard rolls	From $8.50 per 100 sheets

*Prices quoted are for the smallest size and quantity available for purchase, rolls are more economical.

involving heat. No document or artifact should ever be laminated. Never encapsulate artifacts with powdery surfaces, such as pastels, charcoal, or chalk, as the static of the polyester will destroy the image. Static from polyester will also cause additional damage to artifacts with flaking paint.

In preparation for framing or storage, paper and parchment artifacts are often matted or mounted. In many instances, this is done improperly and causes additional damage rather than protecting the work of art. The boards used for matting and mounting are not always up to conservation standards. Just because a framer offers a board, it should not be assumed that it is adequate for your artifact.

Poor quality boards are acidic and can cause **matt burn** — a darkening where the board touches your artifact. Matt burn weakens the paper and causes it to become brittle. Always specify that you would like an acid-free, 100 percent rag, conservation-quality board. Ask to see the board and confirm the maker and grade.

There are many framer's tapes, adhesives, and methods of adhering your artifact to the mounting board. Never use pressure-sensitive adhesive tapes, heat-activated adhesives, or "dry mounts" to attach your artifact to the mount board. These methods can discolour or stain your object, cause deformations, result in breakages as your object expands and contracts with environmental fluctuations, cause your object to become brittle, or weaken your artifact. These adhesives are difficult, if not impossible, to remove. Your artifact should never have an adhesive applied completely over the reverse or on all perimeter edges; it should be hinged at the top edge only (see Appendix 10: Matting and Framing Paper Artifacts).

Matts and mounts applied by an artist are historically and aesthetically important. They should be maintained and, if possible, incorporated into the new mounting package. If in doubt, find someone to consult prior to taking action.

When to Call a Conservator

Maintaining a collection means that with time you probably will encounter damage and problems that require the attention of a conservator. It is important to know when you should call on a specialist.

Buckling and Deformation from Plane

When parchment, vellum, and other hides begin to buckle due to high humidity or exposure to moisture, the fibres of the tissue that form the structure are losing their directionality due to a loss of tension. Some buckling is expected and, if it is minimal and does not interfere with the aesthetic appeal of the work, it may not need immediate professional treatment but may need some preventative care at home. If the deformations do affect the visual appearance of the work or are causing the paint or other decoration to flake, you should consult a conservator. The same is true for paper artifacts.

Water Damage: Tide Lines, Mildew, Mould

Tide lines occur as water and impurities are wicked through paper or other support and impurities are left behind as the water evaporates. Tide lines should be referred to a conservator since trying to remove them could result in additional movement of the impurities.

Parchment is extremely sensitive to water and moisture. Therefore any stain removal, cleaning, or repair of tears should be referred to a conservator.

Mildew refers to a specific kind of mould or fungus, usually related to agriculture, that has a powdery or downy appearance. But the term is generically used to refer to mould growth that has a flat profile.

Mould is always present in the air. Given the right environmental conditions, it will begin to grow on any suitable surface: glues; sizing applied to paper or clothes; paper; and invisible oily fingerprints. Mould colonies grow in many colours, from bright pastels to black, and are sometimes hard to detect. Often a musty odour first indicates the presence of mould or mildew. If the mould growth has not progressed too far into the structure, it can be brushed off, but this is not prudent as the spores can enter your lungs and colonize. Mould is a health hazard as well as a hazard to your artifact and should be referred to a conservator.

Tears, Breaks, and Losses

Tear, breaks, and losses should always be repaired by a conservator. Never try to fix these problems with tape or adhesive as this will often lead to additional damage and a more costly and difficult treatment later. Damaged items should be treated by a conservator but can be encapsulated or stored in an acid-free folder so that no pieces are lost until conservation treatment is possible.

Stamps

Adhesive backed stamps should be handled with great care. The humidity and oils on fingertips can easily disturb the surface of the adhesive. Always wear gloves and use wide-tipped tweezers to move stamps.

The adhesive on the back of many stamps is susceptible to high humidity that can cause the adhesive to stick to adjacent materials. Do not hinge or mount previously unused stamps with adhesives. This will lower the value of the stamp.

Many stamp collector supply houses offer photocopy protection pages, pages that prevent copying of the stamps, and black mounting pages. Tests have shown that many of these pages are acidic and will cause damage and discolouration of the stamps with long-term exposure.

Stamp storage should be uncoated polyester, acid-free buffered paper, glassine, or parchment paper. Polyester sleeves can be stored in a three ring binder, some of which "zip" open down the side for easy access and to allow viewing of both sides of the stamp. There are mounts for individual stamps that require no adhesive. Once mounted, stamps can be stored in an acid-free box.

Trading cards

There are different grades of trading cards. Common cards that are purchased in packs have a low monetary value. Popular cards that are collected because of the card image or information also are of little monetary value. Premium cards are ones that have a monetary value of over five dollars. The most valuable are sets that have been left in their original factory packaging.

Usually common cards are stored in boxes. Acid-free boxes are recommended since you never know when a common card may become valuable. Sets are also usually stored in boxes. When you buy a set, it is usually sealed in a printed Mylar (Melinex) envelope or sealed in plastic. Sets should be handled infrequently and with care. You should wear gloves because damage to the plastic or the image printed on the Mylar lowers the value of the set.

Popular and premium cards are usually stored in sleeves. There are sleeve pages that hold two to nine cards that fit into binders. There are also sleeves for single cards that would then be stored in an acid-free box. There is a wide range of different materials and quality sleeves available. It is important to insure that you are storing your trading cards in polyester sleeves. Sleeves should be acid-free, and plastic sleeves should not contain PVC. Again, always wear cotton gloves when handling premium cards.

CHAPTER 3

Books

In order to care for a book collection, it is important to understand a bit about the construction and structure of books. The text of a book, the combined printed or written pages of a book, is determined by the orientation of the text on a page, whether the paper is folded to form multiple pages, and, if so, how many times they are folded.

Unfolded paper results in two pages (**leaves**), front and back, per sheet of paper. These sheets can be put together, or **bound**, in several ways: glue/adhesive, sewing, staples or posts, oriental binding, or ring or spiral binders.

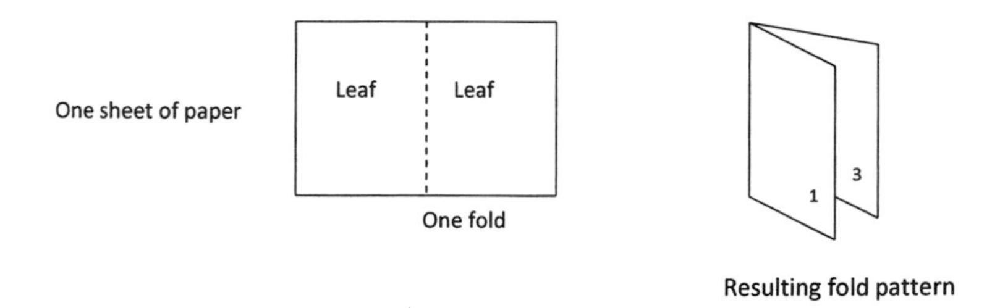

Diagram 2:
Sheets and leaves

A sheet of paper can be printed on both sides and then folded one or more times. The folded form is called a **signature** or gathering.

- One sheet, folded once = 2 leaves = 4 pages
- One sheet, folded twice = 4 leaves = 8 pages
- One sheet, folded three times = 8 leaves = 16 pages. This is the most common format and it is called an octavo.

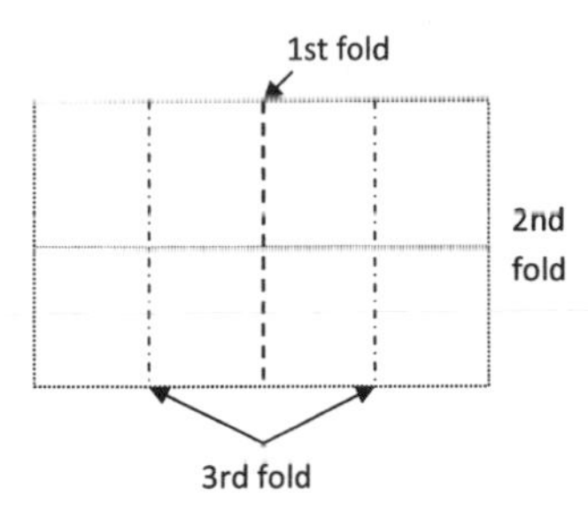

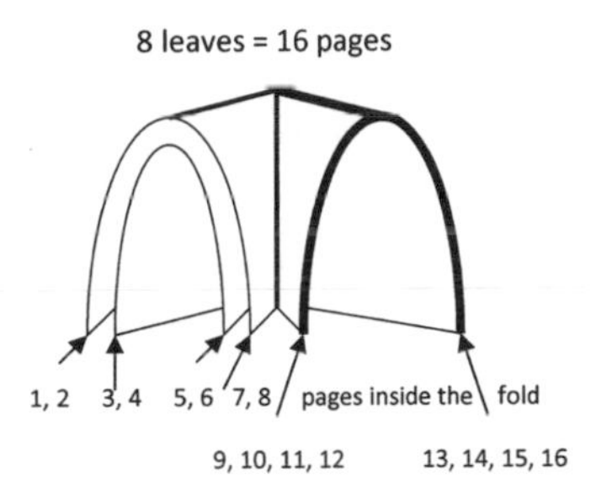

Diagram 3:
Folds and leaves in an octavo

Folded signatures are bound together either by sewing a continuous thread along the inside of the fold that comes out as a chain stitch on the **spine** or by a thread coming out of the fold and wrapping around a cord or tape placed perpendicular to the spine. Sewing causes a slightly thicker block at the spine.

Bound pages are called a **text block**. Once the **end sheet** or **end paper** is added the text block becomes a **book block**. Adhesive is applied to the spine to help with alignment and the block is trimmed to open all the folds in the sheets.

The spine is shaped with a slight curve away from the text to help reduce the bulge at the spine caused by sewing. The spine is then lined with cloth and, sometimes, additional reinforcements.

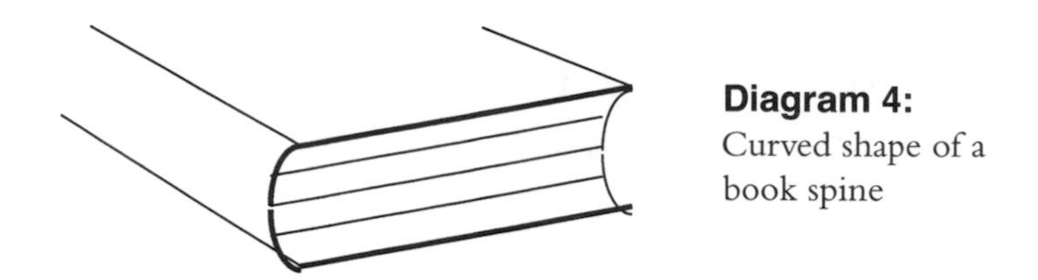

Diagram 4:
Curved shape of a book spine

In early bindings and in some hand bindings today, the boards are laced onto the book block and then covered with leather or fabric. In most bindings today, the cover boards and cloth or leather are put together first then adhered to the book block. This is called case binding.

In a paperback book, the folded edges of the spine are usually not sewn but are ground away, adhesive is applied, and the soft cover is glued on. The glue used for older paperbacks is prone to drying out, leading to loose pages.

Preservation Concerns

Books are sensitive to all the environmental factors already considered: light, temperature, relative humidity, and infestation (mould, insects, or rodents). One important factor in the deterioration of leather bindings is air pollution. The absorption of chemical air pollutants, especially sulphur dioxide from car exhaust, accelerates the breakdown of the natural oils and fats in leather, causing bindings to crack with normal handling. There are many abrasive particles present in the air; these particles land on the books causing deterioration of the exposed edges of the paper and bindings, staining, and abrasion.

It is easy to damage a bound volume through poor handling. Removing a book from the shelf by pulling at the top of the spine (**head cap**) results in damage and tearing of the binding.

Books with damaged spines or failing bindings need adequate support when being handled to prevent separation of the book block from the binding. Additional handling recommendations can be found in Appendix 4: General Rules for Handling and Moving Artifacts and Works of Art.

The information in books may need to be shared among several people, but photocopying a book is discouraged. Most photocopiers require that a book be open to lay flat at 180 degrees. This can fracture the spine of the book, crack older or **desiccated** (dried out) adhesives, and break the stitching of older bindings, causing pages to loosen or fall out. If you have to make photocopies, it is important to make one copy onto a permanent durable paper using an electrostatic copier with edge platens that allow books to be copied at 90 instead of 180 degrees. Additional copies can be made from this high quality master.

Preventative Conservation of Books

The first step is always to thoroughly examine your book to check for damage, potential problems, and the overall structural stability of the work. One of the most helpful things that can be done at home is good housekeeping. Thoroughly dust the books and storage area and inspect for mould and insect infestation at least once every 12 months.

Surface dirt should be removed not only to improve the aesthetics of the book but also to eliminate a hazard. Dirt is abrasive, it may be acidic, and it holds moisture that promotes the growth of mould spores. A very light, dry surface cleaning will reduce the amount of dust, fibres, and other foreign materials that may have collected on the surface of the books.

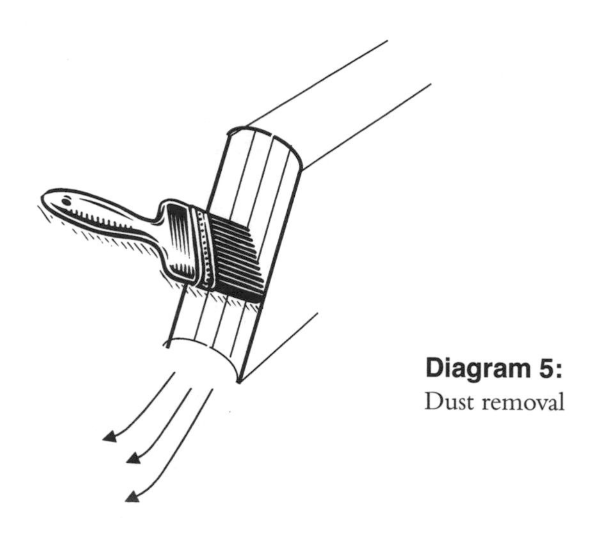

Diagram 5:
Dust removal

Wearing white cotton gloves, begin by gently blowing away any loose surface dirt with an air bulb. Then brush lightly with a soft natural bristle brush or a soft, lint free cloth. (Old shaving brushes are great for this. Just make sure they are clean and dry.) Holding the book firmly closed, begin brushing from the spine of the book in a downward motion toward and off the open edge of the book block. Use very light pressure; the pages should not move with your brush strokes.

Another way to remove accumulated dust is with a vacuum cleaner. Using the brush attachment, place a piece of cheesecloth between the brush attachment and the hose to prevent pieces of lose binding or paper from being sucked into the vacuum. With the same motion as used with a brush, clean the book block moving away from the spine. If small pieces are caught in the cheesecloth they should be saved in a small Melinex envelope for structural conservation in the future.

After brushing and vacuuming to remove loose dust and debris, additional cleaning with a combination of erasers and eraser powders can reduce any remaining surface dirt and grime (see Appendix 6: Surface Cleaning Books). Once the surface dirt has been reduced, the book can be prepared for storage or display.

Storage and Display of Books

Storage and display of books are often one and the same. When choosing shelving for books, you should avoid uncoated wood since it emits acid gases that damage bindings and paper. Wooden shelves should be sealed with paint. Do not use Varathane or other oil-modified polyurethane varnishes or oil paint. These products release corrosive materials as they dry and age. Other products to be avoided are alkyd paints, varnishes, one-compound epoxy esters, anti corrosive paints, alkyd baking enamels, and most wood stains. If transparency is not an issue, coat wood with acrylic or vinyl acrylic latex after sealing any knots with shellac. Allow shelving to dry for at least one month before storing books. If you

> Teak shelving has two drawbacks as a support for paper and other acid deteriorated artifacts.
>
> 1. It contains Tectoquinone (ß-methyl-antraquinone), a volatile crystal that gives off tectonic acid.
> 2. The same oily feel and residue that make teak a durable and long-lasting wood for outdoor use can migrate and cause staining and increased rapid deterioration of cellulose-based artifacts.
>
> You would never want to paint teak but you should isolate any books displayed on teak shelving with a layer of Melinex behind and below the books or with a sheet of acrylic (Plexiglas) or glass to limit contact with the wood.

desire transparency, you could line the shelves with either Melinex polyester laminate or Plexiglas acrylic sheets that may reduce acid transfer. However, there has been no long-term testing of these methods to determine if they do act as a sufficient barrier.

Keep books away from radiators and vents; the heat dries adhesives in the bindings and the leather. The use of humidifiers or trays of water near heat sources in winter and dehumidifiers in summer may help to stabilize the overall relative humidity in your home. Store and display books away from heating/cooling and plumbing pipes.

You might want to display the books in your collection that are important or frequently used. When displaying books, pay attention to adequate support of the binding structure and to the environmental conditions discussed earlier. Do not display books upright with the covers open. The weight of the book block can damage the binding because of the difference in height between the book block and the **square**.

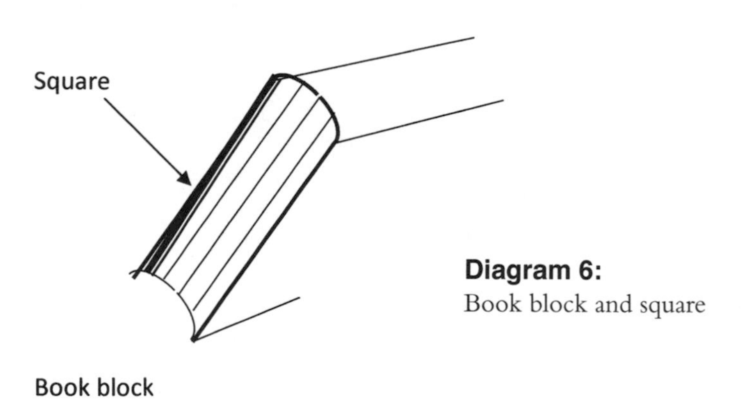

Diagram 6:
Book block and square

A book *can* be displayed on an angle if adequate support is given to the block. You can make a simple angled support or cradle to display books on an angle. One size support can be used to display many sizes of books (see Appendix 7: Angled Supports for Displaying Books). Many archival suppliers sell angled supports fabricated from Plexiglas acrylic.

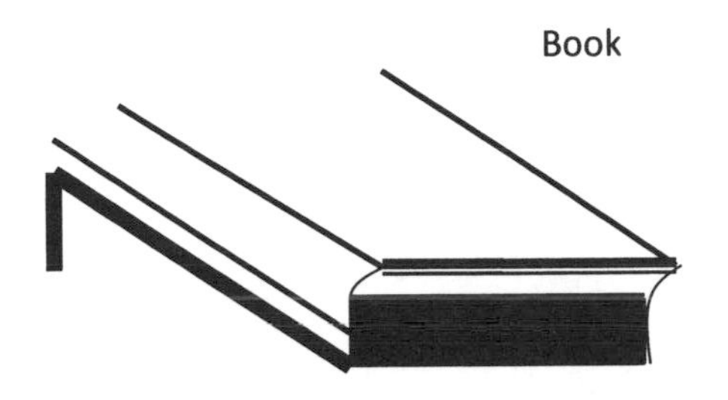

Diagram 7:
Angled display

French or gallery easels have two small pieces that wrap around the bottom of the book to the front, used for display of small prints, paintings, and plates are not recommended for books. It is not advisable to use easels constructed from wood or metal.

Diagram 8:
Side view of a French easel

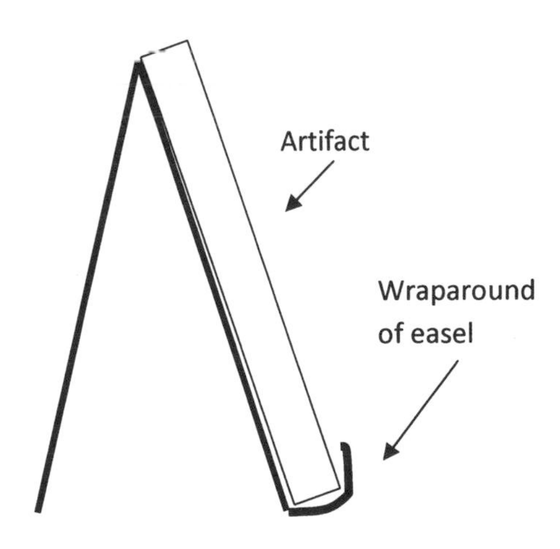

Displaying a book in the open position is also discouraged. Environmental damage during prolonged display can be detrimental to the page. For short-term display or while referring to a volume, you should use a V-shaped support. V-shaped supports can be inclined or flat and can be purchased from an archival supplier or constructed. A simple V-shaped support can be formed from a pillow or wedges of Ethafoam (polyethylene foam) covered in cotton.

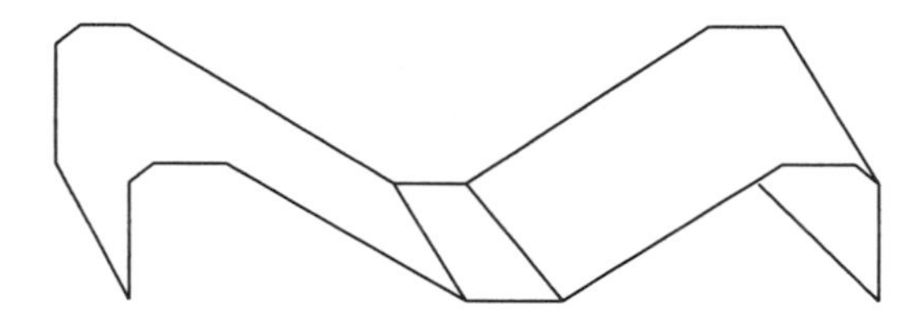

Diagram 9:
V-shaped supports

When to Call a Conservator

Damages to books are quite varied and can include stains, split endpapers, failing bindings, or desiccated adhesives. The most common damage includes broken joints resulting in a loose or free book block (no longer attached to the binding), loose or free pages, tears, broken bindings, or broken boards. Never use pressure-sensitive tape (carpet tape, masking tape, transparent tape) to repair a book or document. Pressure sensitive tapes cause staining and become brittle with time. The removal of pressure sensitive tape can damage your artifact and should be referred to a conservator. Although most damages should be referred to a conservator, some of them can be temporarily dealt with at home.

Broken joints, loose or free book blocks, and loose or free pages should be temporarily secured to assure that no portion of the book is lost. There are three primary methods to secure pieces of a volume together.

For temporarily securing a volume that is not frequently used:

1. Wrap the volume with acid-free paper and tie the package with a soft piece of twill tape or soft, unbleached cotton ribbon.

For volumes that are used more frequently:

2. From quilted cotton fabric make a book "cozy" that ties closed on all four sides (see instructions Appendix 8: Making a Book Cozy).
3. Purchase or construct a box to store the damaged book (see Appendix 9: Construction of Folders and Book Boxes).

Pamphlets can be treated in a similar manner as books. Since pamphlets are less than 1½ cm thick and do not have a rigid cover, they usually need additional protection. Pamphlets can be stored in boxes, folders (see Appendix 9: Construction of Folders and Book Boxes), or be encapsulated in Melinex (see Appendix 5: Encapsulation Process).

CHAPTER 4

Paintings and Other Framed Works of Art

Preservation Concerns

Environment

As with all collections, the environment affects the long-term preservation of oil paintings and other framed artifacts (see Table 3: Environmental Recommendations for Framed Artifacts). A relative humidity of 45 to 55 percent RH is recommended but is very difficult to maintain in Canada during the winter. If a humidifier or humidistat is used, it should be set between 35 and 40 percent in the winter and 50 and 55 percent in the summer to help control seasonal fluctuations.

Caring for and maintaining framed works requires knowing which support materials the artist chose, usually canvas (fabric), wood, or paper. Artists, especially contemporary artists, use many other support materials, such as metal, glass, and plastics. The problems encountered with these paintings should immediately be referred to a conservator. The care of framed watercolours, pastels, and other paper-based artifacts can be better understood if you read the section on paper and books.

Table 3:

Environmental Recommendations for Framed Artifacts

Type of object	Recommended Relative Humidity	Recommended Temperatures	Recommended Light Levels
Oil Paintings	45–55%, above 65% promotes mould growth	18–20°C (65–68°F), never above 25°C	150 lux
Framed Paper, water-colours, pastels, etc.	40–50%	18–21°C (60–70°F)	No more than 50 lux
Painting on unprimed canvas or fabric	45–55%, > 65% intake of moisture increased rapidly 68–70% promotes mould growth	18–21°C (60–70°F)	No more than 50 lux
Photographic materials	30–45%	18–20°C (65–68°F)	50–100 lux colour photos 100–200 lux black and white

Handling, storage, and display cause much of the damage to framed works of art. See Appendix 4: General Rules for Handling and Moving Artifacts and Works of Art, for proper handling and general care procedures. Frames do not protect artifacts and can, in fact, damage an artifact if the frame is inadequate, the artifact is installed in the frame improperly, the hanging hardware is insecure, or the frame is mishandled.

Preventative Conservation

The cleaning of framed works can be quite hazardous. Unglazed artifacts (pictures not protected by glass) should not be cleaned or dusted at home. Never touch the surface of an unglazed picture. Never try home remedies to "brighten" or clean the surface of a painting, especially the "picture cleaners" offered by antique dealers or framers. The chemicals in these cleaners can damage the surface of the painting and the additives remain on the surface causing on-going deterioration.

Original picture frames are part of the artifact. Care should be taken when handling them (see Appendix 4: General Rules for Handling and Moving Artifacts and Works of Art). Older frames are very vulnerable at the corners and the ornamentation is often fragile. Never discard an older frame just because it is damaged or not to your liking. Having an original frame for a work of art often raises its historic and monetary value.

Dust tends to get trapped in frame ornamentation. If there are no visible losses and the surface is not flaking, you can dust a frame lightly. Do not use a cloth or feather duster. Either can easily catch on frame ornamentation and cause damage. Always start at the top of the frame and work toward the sides and down. Dust with a very soft bristled brush. You can hold a vacuum nozzle a few centimetres from the surface to collect the dust lifted by the brush. The vacuum should *never* come in direct contact with the surface of the frame.

The glazing of framed artifacts often needs cleaning. If the glazing material on your artifact is not glass, it is important to use the appropriate cleaning method. If the glazing is just dusty, it can be wiped with a dry cloth. Grime on the surface of plain glass can be removed using a cloth dampened with plain water or water with a small amount of vinegar or another mild solvent added. Cleaning acrylic (Plexiglass), Denglas, UV filtering glass, and many other glazing materials requires special solvents. The cleaning solvent should be applied to the cloth. *Never* spray anything directly onto the glazing. The spray can damage ornamentation and the surface finish of the frame or it can get trapped between the glazing and the rebate (frame edge), wick into the artifact, and promote mould growth.

Storage

Framed works are always safest when stored hung. If that is not possible, it is important to store paintings in the most stable and secure environment possible. Attics experience extreme fluctuations in temperature and unfinished basements are often quite damp. An unused closet or a space in a spare room may best serve the artifacts. If the storage can be darkened by pulling the shades and closing the door, this is beneficial. If the framed works are to be stacked against a wall for an extended period, they should be stacked face to face and back to back and covered to prevent dust accumulation. Never place frames directly on uncarpeted floors. Support pads can be made from old towels or by flattening a thin roll of paper towels. Place two pads perpendicular to the wall to protect the bottom of the frames. Stacks of framed works should be kept shallow — two or three frames only. Secure stacks with weights to prevent slipping or tilting away from the support wall.

Diagram 10:
Stacking paintings

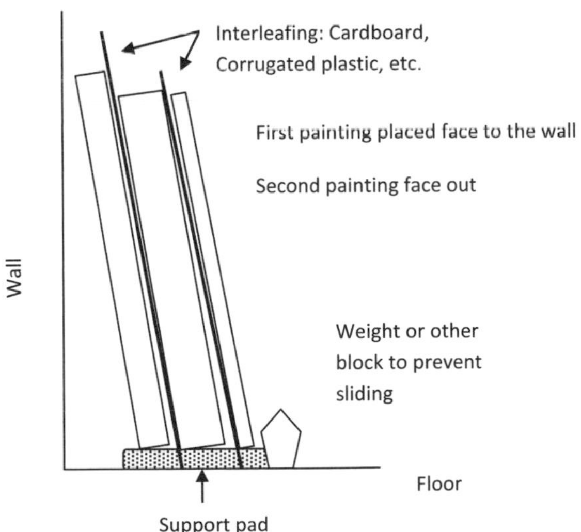

Display

Never hang artifacts above a fireplace, heat register, radiator, baseboard heater, humidifier, or air conditioner vent. Do not hang framed artifacts on an uninsulated wall. Condensation can form between the wall and the back of the painting promoting the growth of mould and micro-organisms. All framed artifacts should have a backing board. Backing boards strengthen the frame and buffer the back of the painting from environmental fluctuations.

Secure the frames to the wall using a ring hanger, often referred to as a D-ring, or screw eyes on both sides of the reverse of the picture frame with corresponding wall hooks. D-rings are preferable to screw eyes. Screw eyes can loosen with the tension of supporting the weight of the painting since they are installed perpendicular to the stress.

Picture wire is not recommended because wire can rust, it weakens with time, and excess wire can damage the back of the painting. If you have to use wire, you should replace old wire and hardware. Attach ring hardware to the frame at approximately one-third of the total height of the frame measured from the top. It is easiest to tie one side of the wire to the ring then pull the wire to the other side.

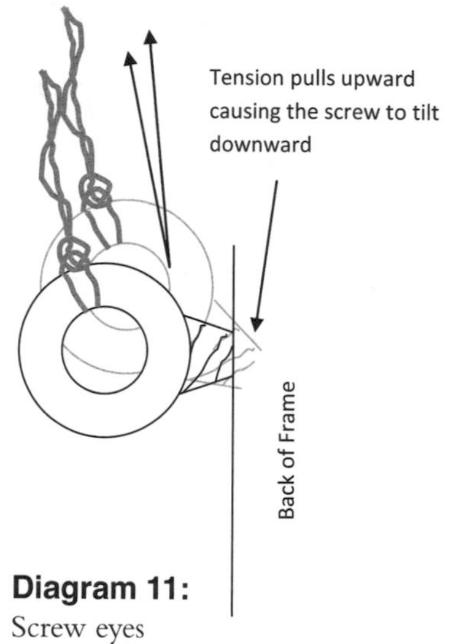

Diagram 11:
Screw eyes

Wire should be looped twice through the ring. A knot is made by looping one wire under the other (the same as starting to tie a shoelace). The wire should be pulled fairly taut across the back of

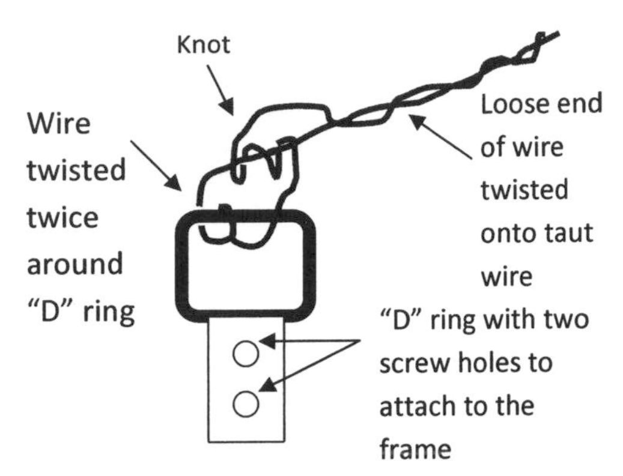

Diagram 12:
Securing wire to ring hardware

the picture frame; it should not be slack. The loose wire ends are then twisted around the taut wire.

When to Call a Conservator

Frame Damage

If the surface finish of a frame gets damaged, you should not attempt to repair or retouch the damage. Never repaint a gilded frame. There are several gilding techniques, and the various techniques are easily affected by many paint media. If the surface is aesthically unpleasing and it is an original frame, consult a conservator. If treatment of the damage is not possible at this time, label the frame and store it adequately. Use a temporary frame to display the artifact, noting on the back of the temporary frame where the original frame is stored.

If pieces of gesso, plaster, or wood ornamentation fall off a frame, keep them, labelled and stored, until a conservator can reattach the losses using appropriate methods. Trying to glue broken pieces onto a frame can often cause additional damage and not be aesthetically successful. Reversal of home repairs is tedious and often costs more than the original repair would have.

Glazing can break, **craze**, cloud, scratch, or become otherwise damaged. As long as the shards have not cut or become embedded in the artifact, replacing the glazing can be done at home or by a framer following the guidelines in Appendix 10: Matting and Framing Paper Artifacts.

Bucking and Deformations from Plane

A framed artifact can buckle or distort from plane when exposed to high humidity or moisture. Frames offer some protection from environmental fluctuations, but prolonged exposure to extremes will affect the artifacts. If a painting on canvas or wood has deformations, it should be immediately referred to a conservator. If the deformations affect the visual appearance of the works on paper or textiles, or are causing the paint or other decoration to flake, consult a conservator.

Water Damage: Mould, Mildew, Tide Lines

Mould is always present in the air. Given the right environmental conditions, it will begin to grow on any suitable surface: glues, sizes applied to surfaces, clothes, paper, wood, and invisible oily fingerprints. Mould colonies grow in many colours, from bright pastels to black, and are sometimes hard to detect. It is often a musty odour that indicates the presence of mould or mildew. If the mould growth has not progressed too far into the structure, it can be brushed off, but this is not prudent as the spores can enter your lungs and colonize. Mould is a health hazard as well as a hazard to your artifact and should be referred to a conservator.

Tide lines occur as water and impurities are wicked through a fibrous structure and the impurities are left behind as the water evaporates. Tide lines are often difficult to detect on a painted surface but can often be seen clearly on the reverse of a painting. Any exposure to water resulting in tide lines should be referred to a conservator. Trying to remove tide lines could result in additional movement of the impurities, and, if an artifact has been exposed to sufficient water, underlying layers of the structure could be damaged.

Tears, Holes, Flaking,

Tears, breaks, and losses should always be repaired by a conservator. Never try to fix these problems with tape or adhesives as this will often lead to additional damage and a more costly and difficult treatment later. Any flakes or loose pieces should be saved until conservation treatment is possible.

CHAPTER 5

Still and Moving Pictures

Almost every family has a collection of photographs and movies. The images may be antique or more recent. The collection may include varied photographic materials ranging from negatives, prints, albums, miniatures, images in cases or frames, to digital photos and videos. The photograph may be the most tangible thing many family historians collect. Photographs allow a glimpse into the past and link us with our ancestors and living relatives.

There are many materials and techniques used to produce photographs, but all photographs have the same basic structure of a support layer and an emulsion layer. It is the emulsion layer that captures the image. Supports are usually paper, glass, or film (think of negatives), but numerous other supports have been used such as metal, fabric, wood, china, plastic, and stone to name a few.

Preservation Concerns

Glass Supports

Glass has been used to support both negative and photographic images. A glass support has an emulsion applied to the surface. The emulsion is either for creating a negative or to produce a photographic image. Glass does not expand or contract — it is dimensionally stable, but it poses some real concerns for long-term care. It is fragile and creates a hazard when it breaks. Glass is heavy, and the emulsion layer applied to the surface can easily separate from the smooth surface of the glass. Many historic images have been lost because of the problems with glass. It is strongly recommended that, if you have any images on glass, you have them duplicated.

Paper

The quality of a paper support affects the stability of the image. Fibre-based paper and water-resistant/resin-coated papers are the most common in home collections. Fibre-based papers were introduced in the early nineteenth century and, from 1839, rag fibres were used to produce a higher quality fibre-based paper.

Paper has a strong affinity for moisture. Humidity and exposure to water cause dimensional changes in the paper structure, which often differs from dimensional changes in the image layer and results in damage as the swelling and shrinking cycle progresses. Curling and other deformations are common in fibre-based paper prints. In the 1940s, resin coated papers were introduced to reduce the problems with moisture absorption in papers. Both resin-coated and fibre-based papers are still in use.

The emulsion layer is the surface coating that holds the image. The emulsion layer of either fibre-based or resin-coated paper can crack if not cared for adequately. Deterioration is a result of high light levels, large fluctuation of the relative humidity, prolonged RH cycling, or high temperatures. Exposure of the paper and emulsion to different environmental conditions, especially varying humidity levels, is a frequent cause of damage. Two common situations can result in damage:

1. When a photograph is framed but the back of the frame is not sealed, the emulsion is buffered from environmental changes by the frame glass but the support paper is unprotected from the reverse and continues to expand and contract with changes in the environment.
2. When a photograph is stored face up (unframed) and the paper backing is buffered by the material on which it is lying, the emulsion is unprotected.

Film

Film is a generic term used to describe a wide variety of flexible, transparent supports. Nitrate, acetate, and polyester have been used as film supports. Nitrate films were introduced in late 1880 and were phased out by the 1950s. These films should be stored apart from your collection and in a cool location, not in a hot attic or garage. They are chemically unstable and can spontaneously ignite. If you find nitrate film in your collection, contact a conservator to arrange for the safe printing of the images and destruction of the film.

Acetate film can fade and discolour. The acetate can shrink and the film layers separate or "wrinkle." These problems are accelerated with exposure to harsh environmental conditions. Polyester films are more permanent than acetate. They are less brittle and dimensionally more stable

Due to the instability of photographic materials, it is prudent to make copies of historic or significant images. Consult a conservator or archivist prior to making duplicates to find an appropriate photographer and processor to assure the safety of your originals and the longevity of your duplicate images. Whenever you make copies of photographic materials, request two copies: one for display, reference, and handling, and a second for dark storage.

Digital Images

Digital images are quickly replacing negative-based photography and movies. As technology continues to advance, storage systems for digital images are quickly outdated: from floppy disks and hard drives, to CDs/DVDs, and now memory sticks, cards, and digital frames. It is important that you update the storage method you use for your images so you can retrieve them as technology advances. When compiling your digital images, it is advisable to make two copies, one to access and manipulate as needed and another to be safely stored.

Environmental Concerns for Photographs

Light causes fading of the dyes in the image layers, and extreme temperature changes the speed of the chemical deterioration of photographic materials. Colour images discolour with exposure to light as the dye layers fade. No photographic materials should be exposed to strong daylight. Photographs should be displayed in an area lit by tungsten rather than fluorescent bulbs.

Since temperature and relative humidity are directly correlated, it is important to keep both as stable as possible. The recommended temperature for photographic materials is 18 to 21°C with fluctuations limited to about 5 degrees. Relative humidity should be between 30 percent and 50 percent. Avoid changes and cycles in the RH level since these fluctuations will result in peeling, cracking, and flaking of emulsion layers. Relative humidity levels above 65 percent result in the growth of mould and other micro-organisms. Levels below 25 percent cause brittleness and curling. Most damage to photographic materials occurs at temperatures at or above 25°C, especially when coupled with high RH levels.

The oxidation level of photographic materials is slow in clean air. In cities and other areas of high pollution, oxidation rates increase, causing deterioration of photographic materials. Air purifiers and protective enclosures can slow oxidation rates.

Photographic materials suffer many of the same problems with insects and rodents as paper and textile collections. Fumigants used for infestations could affect the image layers. It is best to try non-chemical methods to control an infestation, if possible.

Handling

Careless handling can easily damage photographic materials. Tears, cracks, losses, scratches or abrasions, stains, and fingerprints can all result from improper handling. Always wear gloves to prevent the transfer of salts and oils from your hands to the emulsion layer. If a photograph is mounted, handle it by the mount. If the mount is original to the photograph and is fragile, use an

auxiliary support, such as an acid-free board, to safely handle the artifact. The rules for unframed paper also apply to photographs and, if the image is framed, the rules for handling framed artifacts apply (see Appendix 4: General Rules for Handling and Moving Artifacts and Works of Art).

Preventative Conservation of Photographic Materials

Storage

Storage materials and enclosures for photographic materials should be made of chemically stable plastic or high quality papers. Avoid acidic papers, envelopes, and boxes. Most papers in our homes and offices are acidic. Other products to be avoided are polyvinyl chloride (PVC) plastic, metal clasps such as paperclips, and rubber bands. Never use tapes or other adhesives near photographs especially the "magnetic" photo albums that have a pre-applied adhesive layer on every page with a plastic sheet that lies over the photograph. The adhesives deteriorate often preventing safe removal of the photographs after only a few years.

Acid-free papers are available **buffered** or **unbuffered**. Buffered papers should not be used with contemporary colour prints or many of the nineteenth century images. Paper enclosures have advantages in that they are opaque, which prevents light exposure, inexpensive, and easy to label with pencil.

Stable plastic enclosures include polyethylene, polypropylene, and uncoated polyester (Melinex). If using plastic enclosures for a photographic collection, it is important to prevent high humidity levels. Exposure to moisture can cause photographic materials to stick to the plastic.

Albums

Albums are a very popular way to store photographs. Albums should be made of acid-free archival materials. Coloured album pages, even if acid-free, should be avoided as the dyes used can cause deterioration.

Historic Albums

Historic albums present us with a conundrum. Most historic albums are not made from archival grade materials. Low-grade albums affect the long-term preservation of the photographic materials that they house. Historic albums are themselves a piece of history. Photographs were chosen and arranged in a particular order representing a point of view. Within albums we often find notations, dates, and other information of historic significance. Although historic albums are not the best method to store photographic materials, it is felt by many that photographs removed from their album lose part of their historic significance, so historic albums are treated as artifacts.

Historic albums that do not have interleaves should have interleafing sheets added at each page. Since the majority of the materials used to construct these albums are highly acidic, it is recommended that a thin sheet of unbuffered paper be used. It is essential that the interleafing be thin enough not to stress the spine of the album by adding too much thickness.

Display

Photographs can be displayed in the same manner as any paper artifact. Follow the guidelines for matting and framing outlined in Appendix 10: Matting and Framing Paper Artifacts. Long-term exposure to light can discolour image layers. Make duplicate images of items to be displayed and store one image in dark storage, or regularly rotate the images on display.

Cased Photographs

Case photographs, such as miniatures, daguerreotype, ambrotype, and some tintypes, are mounted in small padded cases with a metal matt and glass covering. These cases should not be opened to remove the photograph. If there is a problem, it should be immediately referred to a conservator.

When to Call a Conservator

Photographs are multiplayer constructions that are quite complex structurally and chemically. There is not much that can be done in the home for photographs other than providing stable environmental conditions and adequate storage and display.

If photographic materials are damaged, you should always contact a conservator. If treatment is not possible at this time, the material may be encapsulated or stored in an envelope until treatment is possible.

Projection Films

From 1893 to 1951 film was produced from cellulose nitrate, which is flammable. These films should be stored apart from your collection and in a cool location, not in a hot attic or garage. They are chemically unstable and can self-ignite. If you find nitrate film in your collection, contact a conservator to arrange for the safe printing of the images and destruction of the film. Around 1951 cellulose acetate film, also referred to as "safety film," was introduced to replace the flammable nitrate-based film.

Acetate film degradation, commonly known as "vinegar syndrome," is an inherent vice in the chemical composition of the plastic film support. The signs include a strong vinegar-like smell and shrinkage of the plastic. The film becomes brittle and the shape becomes distorted. The rate of deterioration depends greatly on the storage conditions of the film.

Movies and Slides

The common damage to reeled projection film is from improper threading that results in misaligned sprockets during projection and poor splices. Old splices — repairs of broken films — should be examined regularly for stability and the strength of repair. You can use metal or plastic reels as long as the reel is in good condition and of adequate size. The reel should have a diameter sufficient to leave at least a 1 cm clearance from the outside film layer to the reel edge. Films should have a 1½ metre lead and the film should be evenly wound onto the reel. Poorly maintained equipment can easily damage film. Examine your projection equipment and clean it regularly.

When video cassettes are played or recorded, small magnetic particles flake away. These particles lodge and build up in the player and will cause damage to the video cassette if the machine is not cleaned regularly. Dust and particle build-up are the primary causes of breakage and damage to video cassettes. Video cassettes are a technology that is quickly becoming outdated. To prevent the loss of these films, you should have them transferred onto archival, non-rewritable DVDs.

Technicolour film suffers greatly from fading of the dyes. It is a spontaneous chemical change and nothing can be done to prevent the deterioration. Copying these images and colour correction is often recommended to prevent loss of historical images.

Slides also suffer from colour shift as the dyes fade at different rates. Usually the red dyes fade faster than the yellow, resulting in orange tones. E6 processed slides are more stable and long-term stabilization of the image is possible in storage of 21°C or lower and 40 percent RH or lower. When projecting E6 slides the image should be illuminated for one minute at a time to prevent heat deterioration. Ektachrome slides are less stable and you should not project them for more than 15 seconds.

You should duplicate and colour correct your slide images. To prevent loss of historic images, successive duplication or transferral to other media formats will stabilize a collection and allow for continued use. Colour images should be kept in cool to cold storage with a relative humidity of 40 percent or lower and in the dark.

When handling all film types, always wear white cotton gloves to prevent oil and salt transfer from your skin.

CHAPTER 6

Textiles

The word textile means that the object is made from fibres. Textile constructions include lace, tapestries, household linens, flags, banners, church vestments, hats, fans, nets, dolls, and many more fibre-based materials. Fibres used to create textiles are divided into three main types: synthetic (for example, nylon, polyester), cellulose (for example, linen, cotton), or protein (for example, wool, fur). Fibres can be matted to form felt, pulped to make a paper-like product, or spun to make yarns and threads.

Preservation Concerns

There are many causes of deterioration in textiles. General concerns include light, temperature, relative humidity, and the atmosphere.

- Light, especially ultraviolet light, causes deterioration of the molecular structure and fades applied dyes.
- Heat causes the natural breakdown of the molecule's structure to speed up, causing brittleness, which is especially noticeable in protein fibres such as wool and silk.

- Low RH will also result in brittleness.
- High RH levels result in mould and mildew, and can promote pest infestations.
- Dust and dirt cause damage, especially gritty dirt, which works into the fibres and causes abrasion and breakage.
- An additional concern in urban areas is the sulphur dioxide in the air, a result of pollution, that causes chemical deterioration of the fibres.

Additional forms of deterioration are directly related to the fabrication or construction of the textile; these are referred to as an **inherent vice**. Inherent vices in textiles can be chemical-like problems related to the dyeing process and the applied finishes, or deterioration caused by exposure to solvents.

- The use of certain mordents (fixatives), such as iron, causes deterioration of the fibres and results in small holes.
- Some dyes are unstable and can "bleed" or migrate into surrounding areas upon slight elevations of RH.
- "Weighted" silks are the result of salts added during production, making these fibres very susceptible to moisture and heat. Washing these fabrics is often unsuccessful.

Physical inherent vices are often related to the construction of the textile structure. When fibres are blended, the characteristics of one can result in the deterioration of the other. For example, in a wool-silk blend, wool absorbs moisture, up to one-third by weight, without feeling damp to the touch. Wool needs moisture to prevent it from becoming hard and brittle, but the level of moisture in wool can cause silk to break down. The use of mixed fabrics or the method of construction can cause puckering and deformations (due to constriction and uneven shrinkage at the seams or

Table 4:
Fibre Types and Deterioration Factors

	Acetate and Triacetate	Acrylic	Cotton, linen, and other cellulose fibres	Wool, silk, and other protein fibres	Nylon
Micro-organisms, mould, mildew, fungi	Discolouration	Resistant	Damaged by various micro-organisms	Resistant but micro-organisms tend to attack stains on fibres	Resistant, mildew will attack applied finishes
Insects and pests	Silverfish attack the applied size	Resistant	Moths and beetles do not usually attack cotton but silverfish are attracted to the sizing	Larvae of moths and carpet beetles	Resistant to most insects, roaches will nest in fold and creases
Sunlight	Causes loss of fibre strength	Resistant	Yellows and weakens fibres	Deteriorates fibres	Deteriorates fibres
Heat	Soften with heat (only iron on low and use steam)	Resistant, iron below 161°C	Can scorch with high temperatures	Iron at low temperatures, below 140°C with steam	Soften and discolour at temperatures above 150°C
Fire*	Forms a hard black bead ash	Burns with yellow flame and forms a gummy hot residue	Smells of burning paper and produces a fully grey ash	Self-extinguising when flame is removed, wool forms crisp black bead residue, silk forms a brittle ash	Forms gummy grey/tan ash that hardens when cool, melts away from the flame
Dry cleaning	No problem	No problem	No problem	No problems	No problem
Detergents, surfactants (most are alkali)	Diluted cleaning agents only	No problem	Resistant to alkali	Avoid strong soaps and detergents	No problem

	Acetate and Triacetate	Acrylic	Cotton, linen, and other cellulose fibres	Wool, silk, and other protein fibres	Nylon
Water	Should be handled very carefully, low fibre strength	No problem	Cotton shrinks and deforms	Easily shrinks, can damage applied finishes on silk, especially weighted silks	No problem
Solvents	Acetone, such as fingernail polish remover, will damage the fibres	No problem with weak acids or alkalis	Resistant to most solvents used for stain removal, linen deteriorates with strong acids	Very sensitive to alkali, do not bleach	Resistant to alkali but acids can destroy the fibres
Static	Yes	No	No	No	Yes

* Fire/burn information is given as a means of fibre identification. Burning a small thread can identify a fibre type, which indicates the best long-term care procedure.

applied designs) as a result of the materials reacting differently to the environmental influences. Breakage at creases, pleats, or folds is another common damage related to textile constructions.

Many textiles are attacked by insects. Protein fibres such as wool and silk can suffer from infestations of carpet beetles and moths. The starch finishes applied to cellulose (vegetable) fibres such as cotton and linen can attract silverfish. If you find insects in your textiles you can try freezing to disinfect the items without the introductions of fumigants or toxins (see Appendix 11: Treating Infestations in Textiles by Freezing).

Some of the worst damage and deterioration to textiles is caused by the materials they come into contact with during storage or display. For example, wood is very acidic and causes cotton and linen to darken and become brittle. Often, this is seen as a dark band around the perimeter of a textile that is stretched over a wooden frame for display. In addition to the acid damage caused by the wood, this method of display causes holes from the nails or staples. Nails and staples oxidize (rust) with exposure to moisture or RH, which stains the textile.

Textiles displayed in direct contact with glass can stain or develop tide lines as the condensation that forms on the glass with changes of temperature is wicked through the fibres carrying dirt, grime, or pollutants into the structure of the fabric.

Preventative Conservation of Textiles

Always wash your hands and wear cotton gloves to prevent the transfer of oils from your hands. When handling textiles, make sure you wear no buttons, zippers, necklaces, bracelets, or watches that can catch on the threads or fibres and cause damage (see Appendix 4: General Rules for Handling Artifacts and Works of

Art). It is important to prepare an accession record or inventory with photographs if possible (see Appendix 1: Accession List Information) and examine your textiles for any problems such as damages or insects.

Prior to displaying or storing, remove the dust and dirt by a thorough vacuuming. Use a mesh screen, such as the soft plastic screening sold for windows, and bind or cover the edges with a piece of fabric cloth or ribbon, or seal the edges with masking tape so the screen will not catch on the textile. Place the screen over the portion of the textile to be vacuumed, and pass the hand nozzle of the vacuum over the screen, first in one direction then in the opposite direction. After finishing one section, move the screen to the next area. It is best to work in a grid pattern to assure that the textile is cleaned thoroughly front and back. Special attention should be given to seams, hems, pleats, gathers, and cuffs.

If the textile has never been washed or if the textile has not been washed within the last year, it is always best to refer any

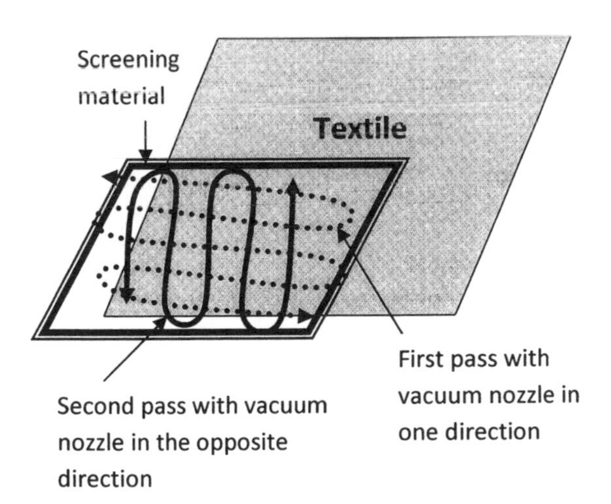

Diagram 13:
Vacuuming a textile

stains, tide lines, discolourations, or overall grime problems to a conservator. There are many things to consider when wet washing or dry cleaning a historic textile. Making the wrong choices could cause permanent and irreparable damage.

Once a textile has been thoroughly vacuumed, you have to decide about storage or display. If a textile is to be stored, most storage decisions are determined by the type and size of the textile. If a textile is small and flat, the best method of storage would be to keep it flat. Flat textiles can be stored in boxes of either acid-free board, stable plastic boxes (see Appendix 15: Some Materials for Preservation by Artifact Type), or other neutral plastic boxes that can add additional protection against insect infestation and moisture fluctuations. Boxes can be purchased pre-made in standard sizes, or constructed at home to the size and shape that best serves the textiles in the storage space available.

Within the box, interleafing sheets of neutral, acid-free, or acid-free buffered tissue or paper should be placed between the textiles. There are many interleafing materials available. Most interleafing papers and tissues are sold either in standard sized sheets or in rolls. To decide which materials would be compatible with a group of textiles, it is important to know the type of fibre used to produce the textile. Neutral and acid-free interleafing can be used with all three types of fibres. Buffered materials offer added protection against the acids produced as a by-product of the fabrication and aging of textiles. Acid-free buffered interleafing should *only* be used with textiles that are 100 percent cellulose fibres. Buffered products can damage protein-based fibres. If in doubt about the fibre type or if faced with a blend of fibres, it is always best to use either an acid-free or neutral product.

Medium sized flat textiles and small three-dimensional textiles such as hats, gloves, or baptismal or christening gowns can be stored boxed if proper precautions are taken to prevent sharp creasing and damage at the folds. Each fold should be stuffed with a crumpled roll or several sheets of either acid-free or acid-free buffered tissue to add cushioning and prevent compression of the folds.

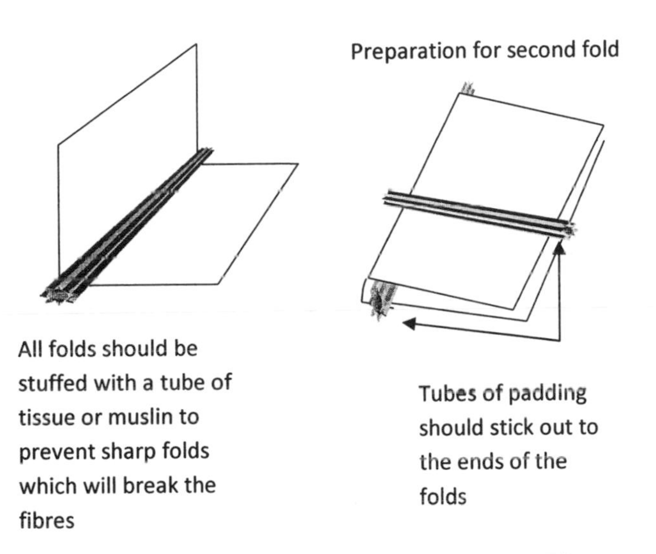

Diagram 14:
Folding small and medium two-dimensional textiles

After folding, the entire object should be wrapped in a layer of tissue and placed in the box. Like objects should be stored together as determined by size, fibre type, or use. If many items are to be stored in one box, label the wrapping tissue of each item in pencil with identification information. Do not put too much weight in each box or the lower textiles will be compressed. Heavy fabrics, or those with embellishments, should be placed below delicate textiles.

Small to medium three-dimensional objects can also be stored folded and boxed. To prepare the textiles, all hats, gloves, muffs, sleeves, collars, and pant legs should be stuffed, as well as any side, shoulder, or inseams. Three-dimensional textiles can be folded to fit in a box if all folds are stuffed with tubes of tissue or muslin to prevent breakage of the fibres. After folding the textiles, wrap in tissue and place in the box.

It is important to list the textiles held in a box on the exterior of the box to reduce handling when searching for a particular item. Use pencil. Never use pens or markers to label boxes or tissue; inks from pens can bleed or transfer. Always use pencil near art and artifacts (see Appendix 4: General Rules for Handling Artifacts and Works of Art). Large, flat, textiles, whenever possible, should be stored rolled. If it can be determined, textiles should be rolled in the warp direction, face out (see Diagram 15). Weft threads form the selvedge edge when they turn over, or re-turn over, the last warp thread. The selvage appears finished and runs the long dimension of the bolt of fabric. The weft threads "fill" the fabric going over and under the warp in a prescribed pattern. The warp threads run the long dimension of the bolt and are cut off the loom at both ends.

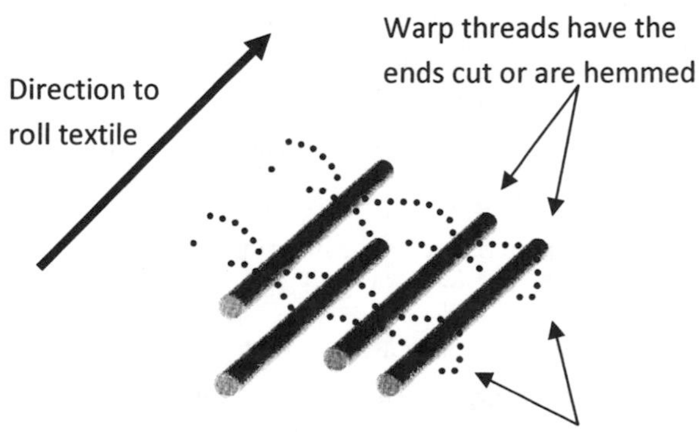

Diagram 15:
Warp and weft

Tubes should be at least 18 cm (sold only in inches — 3 in in this case) in diameter and a minimum of 10 cm wider than the textile. It is best that the tube be acid-free. If it is not, the tube should be covered with a protective layer of Melinex to prevent acid transfer. The outside of all tubes should be covered with a layer of muslin or acid-free tissue prior to rolling the textile onto the tube to help secure the textile in place and allow for easier rolling.

The same piece of muslin or tissue can also be used as an interleafing layer when the textile is rolled. The edges of the textile should align on the tube when the textile is rolled. If a textile has deformations or embellishments or is composed of multiple layers, like quilts, it may be necessary to add padding to the thin areas to keep the roll straight on the tube. Polyester batting can be bunched together and covered with tissue or muslin to form the proper thickness pads. Sometimes this takes some trial and error; it is rare that a textile rolls straight the first time.

After rolling the textile, another piece of muslin or cotton sheeting should be used to cover the tube to protect against dust and dirt accumulation. It is good to mark this outer cover sheet

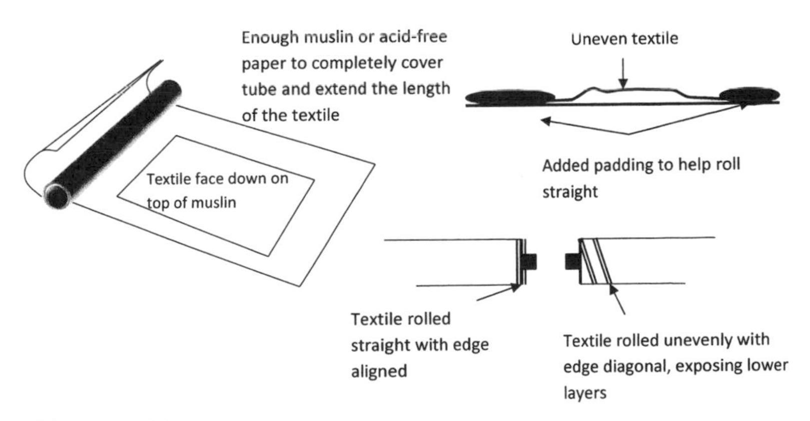

Diagram 16:
Rolling textiles

indicating what textile is inside or attach a photograph to the end of the tube. Marking should only be done in pencil. Uniform sized tubes can easily be hung on chains or ropes to prevent compression of the fibres.

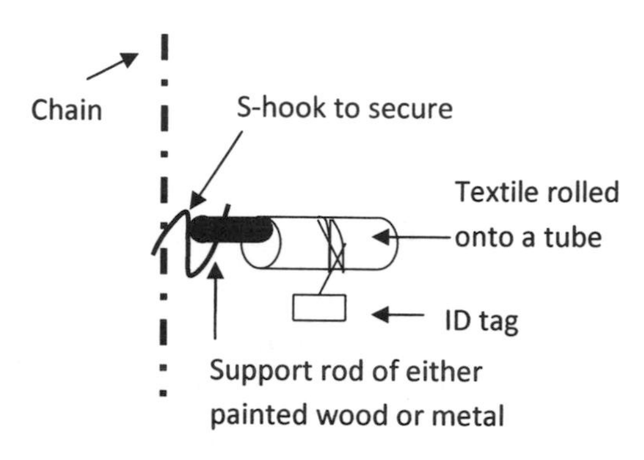

Diagram 17:
Suspending rolled textiles
(View from one end of the rolled textile)

Three-dimensional textiles such as costumes and clothing can be stored either in a box or on a hanger depending on their condition, construction, and size. Most costumes and clothing items can be stored hanging. Hanging the clothing prevents wrinkling and creasing. Items should be hung on padded hangers covered in un-dyed muslin or white cotton sheeting (see Appendix 12: How to Make a Padded Hanger). Do not buy the fancy satin padded hangers. They are expensive and the dyes often transfer with exposure to high humidity. In some instances, it may be necessary to give the artifact added support. You can determine this by hanging the article and observing if there are any areas of stress or pulling. If added support is necessary, stitch a piece of un-dyed twill tape or white grosgrain ribbon into the seam allowance of the area to be supported and tie the other end of the ribbon to the neck of the hanger (see Appendix 12). Dresses or blouses heavily encrusted with beads, pearls, or sequins should not be stored hanging. If there is damage to the artifact, especially at the waist or shoulder, it should be placed in a box. Items that are cut on the bias or knitted should also be stored boxed (see Appendix 13: Boxing Medium to Large Textiles for Storage).

Display

There are three ways to display textiles: hung unframed, mounted and framed, or on a form such as a hat stand or mannequin.

If a textile is to be displayed hanging, have a textile conservator prepare the piece. It is very easy to damage a historic textile by improper stitching, not supporting the weight evenly, or using threads or support fabrics that are incompatible. Framers should not prepare textiles for hanging display.

Three-dimensional textiles can be displayed on an appropriate support. Supports, hat stands, mannequins, and so on should be covered in muslin and well padded so that the textile construction is fully supported.

When Is It Time to Call a Conservator?

Within any collection of textiles, you will probably encounter damage and problems that require the attention of a conservator. Knowing when you should call on a specialist is important.

Deformations from Plane

Textiles can have deformations due to high humidity or exposure to moisture, compression, or tension resulting from the method of construction or the mixing of fibre types. Some deformations are expected and, if they are minimal and do not interfere with the aesthetics, display, or storage of the textile, they need not be professionally treated at this time. Some preventative care at home, added padding during storage, changing the fold locations, or laying a textile flat so folds wrinkles and creases can relax and come to ambient levels of RH may be sufficient to reduce the deformations.

Water Damage

Tide Lines

Tide lines occur as water and impurities are wicked through the textile and the impurities are left behind as the water evaporates. Tide lines should be referred to a conservator since trying to remove them could result in additional movement of the impurities.

Stain removal and cleaning of textiles that were previously unwashed, damaged, or have not been washed in the last year should be referred to a conservator.

Mould, Mildew, and Micro-organisms

Mould is always present in the air. Given the right environmental conditions, it will begin to grow on any suitable surface, such as sizing applied to textile, clothes, uncleaned stains, and residues on the textile surface. Mould colonies grow in many colours, from bright pastels to black, and are sometimes hard to detect. It is often a musty odour that indicates the presence of mould or mildew. If the mould growth has not progressed too far into the structure, it can be brushed off, but this is not prudent as the spores can enter your lungs and colonize there. Mould is a health hazard as well as a hazard to your artifact and should be referred to a conservator.

Tears and Losses

Tears, losses, and separation of seams or other stitch work should always be referred to a conservator. As textiles age and weaken, it is no longer always appropriate to use the same fibre type for stitched repairs. New thread fibres are stronger than older fibres and can easily break or damage the original structure. Conservators can also dye fabrics and threads to match an aged textile. Damaged items should be treated by a conservator but may be encapsulated or wrapped and boxed so that no pieces are lost until conservation treatment is possible.

Flooding

If a textile collection is flooded, move the textiles away from the affected area. Never lift a saturated textile without a support board. The fibres are in a weakened state when wet and can easily break. If a textile is folded, do not try to unfold it. Using support boards, move the textiles to a safe space and lay them on layers of towels or sheets. Place more towels and sheets over the textiles to help with the drying process. If shrinkage is a concern, place light weights on the upper towels to help hold the shape. Increase the air circulation in the space by placing fans blowing indirectly around the textiles. If there is "bleeding" or transfer of dyes, contact a conservator immediately.

CHAPTER 7

Wooden Objects

The variety of wooden artifacts is extensive; furniture, sculpture, and other utilitarian and decorative objects have been made from wood for centuries. There are many methods of production, joining, and finishing wooden products, but the basic preservation principles are the same for all wooden artifacts.

Preservation Concerns

Most damage is a result of inadequate environmental control, water, poor handling, or attacks from insects or bugs.

- Strong light, especially direct daylight, will lighten most woods and can "bleach" applied surface finishes, such as stains and varnishes.
- Oiled woods, sap woods, teak, cherry, and a few other species will darken with exposure to direct sunlight, but surface finishes such as applied varnishes and sealants will still lighten, resulting in a cloudy appearance.
- High temperatures desiccate the wood resulting in cracking.

- High levels of relative humidity cause swelling and cracking of the wood.Veneers release and the glue used in joins can absorb the moisture causing softening, loosening, and failure of the joins. High RH levels allow mould and micro-organisms to flourish.
- Low RH results in wood shrinkage and cracking, veneers shrinking and splitting, and joins failing as the glue become brittle and fails with stress.

Woodworm is a generic term used to describe many wood-boring insects. Furniture beetle (*Anobidae*) and other beetles (*Bostrychide* and *Lyctide*) and termites, are common to wooden artifacts. Clothes moths, silverfish, and carpet beetles are attracted to the upholstery of furniture. Furniture infestations are often hard to detect because of all the joins and crevasses. It is important to look regularly for **frass**, small "puddles" of powder near small holes in the wood caused when the insects exit. Insects can live, and cause damage, in wood for up to five years before exiting an artifact.

Insect infestations in wooden artifacts can spread quickly throughout a whole house. Do not bring new pieces of wood into your home without examining them thoroughly with bright light or flashlights for any sign of exit holes or frass. If you find indications of infestation, isolate the artifact. Place the artifact over a piece of black paper or cloth and completely enclose it in polyethylene plastic sheeting sealed with masking tape (do not let the adhesive tape contact your artifact — it is only used to seal the plastic). Examine all surrounding wooden artifacts to prevent spread of the infestation.

Preventative Conservation for Wood Artifacts

The environmental recommendations for wood are 50 to 60 percent RH and a temperature of 20°C. Gradual changes are more acceptable than quick fluctuations of RH. At RH levels above 65 percent, mould grows and the adhesives used in joins and veneers release.

Cleaning

Vacuum upholstered pieces regularly both from the top and underside. Use compressed air or air bulbs to clean debris from creases and joins. Use microfibre cloth to dust. The threads from regular cloths can easily catch on veneers. Feather dusters are not recommended as the spines can catch on or scratch surface finishes.

Waxing and Polishing

Commercial polishes often have additives, such as silicone, for example, that with time can build up on the surface. These additives can become insoluble and cause discolouration of the applied surface finish or deterioration of the surface coatings. Never use commercially available oils on wood because they either darken as they dry or stay sticky and tacky, which attracts more dust. Especially avoid linseed, lemon, and tung oils. A few times a year, wax unpainted wood surfaces with good quality beeswax, not a silicone wax, using a lint-free cloth. Apply wax sparingly and remove all the excess; more wax is not better. Excess wax attracts dust, streaks, and shows marks, such as fingerprints.

When cleaning composite wooden artifacts that have glass, mirrors, marble, or metal hardware or decorations, take extra care to prevent damage to the different components. When cleaning glass and mirror components, try cleaning the portions closest to the wood with just a dry cloth. If additional cleaning is necessary, do not spray a cleaning solution onto the glass but wet a cloth with water and a few drops of alcohol and wipe. Brass handles, knobs, mounts, and pulls should not be cleaned while attached to the wood. These components must be cleaned with an alkali solution that will damage the surrounding wood and surface finishes.

Do not attempt to clean painted surfaces, such as tables, sculptures, wooden wall hangings, or other decorative items with applied paint. The cleaning of gilded surfaces should be referred to a conservator.

Storage

Wooden artifacts should be stored in areas of low light. Do not store artifacts near pipes that can burst or near heat sources that can cause desiccation. Cover with fabric to allow moisture buffering. Always store furniture and wood artifacts in their proper orientation to prevent stressing joins.

Display

Display wood and furniture away from heat sources and out of direct sunlight. Do not place houseplants on wood, even if the plants have a coaster under them. High humidity from watering plants and the cooling effect of moist soil are likely to damage the wood. Water stains occur frequently when displaying houseplants or flowers in a vase on wood. If you must display flowers, check the vase regularly for leaks by filling it and placing it on a cloth or piece of paper. Cloth will darken slightly with any leaks and small wrinkles or dampness will show on the paper. Always place vases on a cloth or doily placed over a thin piece of plastic. Better yet use silk flowers!

When to Call a Conservator

Frequently, antique wood pieces, especially furniture, have been refinished, which removes all of the original surface finish and any traces of the artifact's history. An original surface finish is an integral part of the artifact and you should attempt to retain the finish. Historical pieces should show their age and history. Special finishing techniques were often used in the past, such as the combed and feathering techniques simulating wood grain patterns that cannot be easily duplicated now. If paint has been applied over an original finish, it is impossible to remove just the top paint layer without special training and experience. Solvents required to remove the paint will remove all the applied finished down to the wood. This problem should be referred to a conservator who can possibly save the original finish.

Flaking or loss of applied surface coating or painted design layer should always be referred to a conservator.

CHAPTER 8

Bone, Horn, and Ivory Artifacts

Ivory comes from elephant tusks but the term is now widely used to describe walrus and narwhal tusks, sperm whale and hippopotamus teeth, and mammoth tusks. Many Canadian collections include Inuit art made with walrus ivory. Bone, horn, and ivory are very similar chemically, but their physical composition and characteristics are different. Ivory is the most sensitive of these materials.

Preservation Concerns for Bone, Horn, and Ivory

The ideal environmental conditions for bone, horn, and ivory are 25°C, 45 to 55 percent RH, and no more than 150 lux of light. All of these artifacts readily react to changes in moisture level and RH levels resulting in swelling and shrinking and, if exposed to frequent or prolonged cycles, cracks and warping occur. With prolonged exposure to light, these artifacts tend to lighten. Darkening in tone is noticeable if these artifacts are frequently handled or worn against the skin, allowing for oils and salts to transfer to the surface of the artifacts. This darkening of utilitarian artifacts is considered the patina and should not be removed but, in future, the items should be handled with gloves.

Bone, horn, and ivory readily stain when in contact with other materials. Do not use rubber bands or metals in contact with these artifacts. If there are metal, leather, or other materials as part of the artifact or mount, they should be sealed or isolated by a conservator to prevent staining and damage.

Insects and rodents are not usually attracted to bone and ivory, but carpet beetle larvae and clothes moths will attack horn.

Preventative Conservation of Bone, Horn, and Ivory

Cleaning

Lightly dust with a soft, lint-free cloth. If there is excessive grime on the surface, wash with a mild soap (not detergent) very diluted in water. Wash a small area with a small sponge or cotton swab. Rinse with clear water and immediately dry. Never submerge a bone, horn, or ivory artifact and do not allow water to stand on the surface for more than minute.

Storage

Tightly sealed drawers, shelves, and boxes offer a buffer against damaging fluctuations in the RH; the darkness protects from light damage. Avoid acidic materials such as wood. Pad shelves with a stable liner such as polyethylene or polyester batting covered in washed muslin or Tyvek to prevent damage. All artifacts react adversely when exposed to polyurethane foams such as those used for inexpensive mattresses, but bone, horn, and ivory are particularly susceptible to damage and staining from polyurethane as it deteriorates.

"French Ivory," sometimes called "India Ivory," is a synthetic material, not an organic animal product like bone, horn, and true ivory. French Ivory was commonly used in the early twentieth century to produce dresser sets and cutlery. Please read about cellulose nitrate in Chapter 9: Plastic and Rubber Artifacts.

Carved teeth, mother of pearl, and tortoise shell artifacts should be treated in much the same manner as bone, horn, and ivory.

When to Call a Conservator

Breaks, losses, flakes, and other damages should be referred to a conservator. Never try to repair a loss or break with adhesives or tapes as it could cause damage to the surrounding area and stain the artifact. Heavy soiling and localized dark discolouration, especially those caused by oxidized metals, should be referred to a conservator.

CHAPTER 9

Plastic and Rubber Artifacts

There are both natural and synthetic rubbers and plastics. Unfortunately, they all start to deteriorate as soon as they are manufactured. The greatest concern with rubbers and plastics is their reaction with oxygen, which changes their composition.

Celluloid Plastic

Plastics have been around since the 1830s. Celluloid, derived from cellulose nitrate, was used widely in the early 1900s for photographic film, picture frames, manicure sets, dresser sets, fashion accessories, and many other decorative items. As celluloid deteriorates the nitrate is released. As the nitrate breaks away, it can be flammable. Moulded celluloid is not as nitrated as film and therefore not as flammable, but caution still should be taken when housing and storing these items. As celluloid deteriorates it turns yellow, shrinks, becomes brittle, emits a bad smell, and produces fragments, powder, or foam residue. The deterioration process releases highly acidic by-products that can affect surrounding materials.

Bakelite

Bakelite is a phenol formaldehyde resin — polyoxybenzl-methylenglycolanhydride — and was the first plastic made from synthetic components. It was developed around 1909 by a Belgian, Dr. Leo Baekeland. Bakelite is known for its heat resistance and non-conductivity. It was used commercially to produce women's accessories, toys, houseswares, and other products, and in industry.

Preservation Concerns

Most plastics are affected by heat, high humidity, and large fluctuations in either the temperature or the relative humidity levels. High temperatures quicken chemical deterioration. Light, especially ultraviolet light, is damaging. Therefore, unfiltered daylight and fluorescent lighting should be avoided. Light should not exceed 150 lux and temperatures should be below 25°C.

Preventative Conservation for Plastic and Rubber

Never use cleaning solvents on plastic. The solvents can react with the plastics and cause deterioration, such as clouding or damage to the surface. If the surface grime requires cleaning with more than a soft dusting cloth, use a soft cloth moistened with room temperature water. A few drops of a mild soap can be added to the water to remove oily grime. Follow up with a rinse cloth.

Storage

The ideal storage for plastic and rubber would be cold, dry dark storage. Oxygen-free storage may be desired for particularly valuable, important, or vulnerable pieces. Proper ventilation is essential to remove deterioration vapours from the area. A conservator can help with designing appropriate oxygen-free storage.

Rubber and plastic artifacts should always be stored in their correct shape and orientation without anything stacked from above or pressure on the sides. Due to the thermoplastic nature of rubbers and plastics, they can easily deform and lose their shape. Never stack, fold, or stress rubbers or plastics for long-term storage.

New plastics, and new uses for plastics, are being developed all the time. In order to best care for plastics in a collection, it is important to know which plastic you have. Since the 1920s, there have been great improvements in the stabilizing additives in rubbers and plastics. Many plastics are relatively new in collections, and studies are still being conducted to determine the optimum conditions for care, storage, and display to slow deterioration of these artifacts.

Consult a conservator for help identifying plastics, and the care, storage, and display of specific plastic or if there is noticeable damage or deterioration.

CHAPTER 10

Glass and Ceramic Artifacts

Most of the problems with glass and ceramics are a direct result of poor environmental controls and improper handling.

Glass

Weeping and **crizzling** are two forms of glass deterioration related to how it was formulated. Glass weep looks like drops of water on the surface of the glass. Weep is a result of moisture penetrating, then being released from the glass structure, carrying some of the glass components with it. With time, the deterioration will cause the surface to look cloudy. The components of weep can damage other artifacts.

Crizzled glass can also develop a cloudy surface, but the damage is the result of a network of cracks on the surface. These cracks may be so fine that they cannot be detected without a microscope.

Ceramics

Ceramics are divided into categories based on their porosity: unfired clay, earthenware or terra cotta, and glazed ware (porcelain and stoneware).

Unfired ceramics are very fragile, water soluble, and easily worn or scraped. Unfired ceramics require special environmental controls and should be handled with extreme caution. Archaeological ceramic artifacts are often unfired.

The glaze of earthenware sits on the surface of the clay body but does not have a strong chemical bond with it. The glazes are applied either decoratively or to waterproof the object. The glaze layer is heated to sufficient temperatures that the silica component of the glaze will melt and bond with the clay body. Earthenware is fired to render it water insoluble but it is still porous and water can penetrate. Earthenware often displays a crackling pattern. Sometimes this pattern is intentional, but often it is the result of a weakness in the glaze "fit" on the body. Weak fit means the glaze did not completely bond to the clay body during firing. As a result of this weak chemical bond, the glaze and the clay react differently to changes in the environment and how it is handled.

Earthenware often suffers from impact and scratches caused by cutlery that can result in losses of the glaze and chips in the clay. If an earthenware ceramic breaks, even if it fits back together, the glaze is likely to have lost small fragments and slivers. Moisture can penetrate into unglazed areas of these ceramics and cause damage, such as cracking of the glazed areas as the trapped water expands with heat.

Porcelain and stoneware are fired at high temperatures. Glazes are bound chemically and physically to the clay, and losses to the glaze layer are not common. Damage to the design usually indicates a layered design process that may or may not have been sealed with a glaze layer over the image. If the image or design on a ceramic piece is applied over the glaze or inadequate glaze is applied over the design, heat and moisture will cause deterioration. Dishwashers or hand washing can cause deterioration but the prolonged exposure to both heat and water in a dishwasher results in damage sooner.

Since many ceramics are utilitarian objects, it is common to see stains. Stains are often irreparable and should be considered part of the aging process. If a ceramic breaks, never attempt to repair it with commercial adhesives, particularly if it will be used to serve food. Many of these adhesives can be hazardous to your health, especially as they deteriorate when warm foods come in contact with them.

Preservation Concerns for Glass and Ceramics

A cause of common problems related to both environment and handling is the practice of warming porcelain dinner plates, which can cause a crackle pattern in the glaze or break or crack the clay body. This damage can also occur if a warm ceramic piece is put into cold water. Ceramics can be damaged by overheating, which causes expansion of the clay that can then break or cause cracking of the glaze. Ceramics can also overheat when displayed near direct sunlight or lit with spotlights, especially incandescent bulbs, which emit a high level of infrared light. Dark coloured glass and ceramics absorb heat more readily than light ones.

Avoid freezing ceramics. Ceramics often retain moisture, which expands when frozen, weakens the ceramic structure, and can cause breakage. This is especially noticeable in terra cotta tiles and exterior bricks.

Ceramics and glass are fairly stable in a wide range of environmental conditions. Relative humidity level recommendations for stable glass and ceramics are 45 to 60 percent RH. Above 65 percent RH, micro-organisms and mould grow. Extreme fluctuations can cause cracks, breaks, and losses of glaze or the clay.

To clean ceramics, remove dust first to eliminate any loose dirt. Use a clean, soft cloth, such as a microfibre, lint-free cloth or a soft bristled brush to loosen and remove dirt from the surface. If the surface is rough or textured, use only a soft brush for dusting. Lint or fibres from a cloth can catch on the ceramic and cause damage.

If there is light grime on the surface that cannot be removed by dusting, you can wipe the surface with a soft cloth slightly dampened with room temperature water. Do not wipe ceramics with paint or decoration applied over the glaze layer, unfired ceramics, or ceramics with damaged glazes. Do not use cleaning sprays, oils, or other solvents, chemicals, or cleaning products.

Sometimes it is necessary to remove oily residue. Line the sink with a towel to prevent damage to the ceramics from accidental bumps against the bottom or the side of the sink. Fill the sink with room temperature water with two or three drops of non-sudsing, low-grade ammonia. Submerge one object at a time, wipe, and transfer to a rinse bath. You might add a few drops of alcohol to the rinse water to promote drying. Air dry the ceramics on a soft towel in an area of good air circulation. Frequently blot the pools of water that form in low areas and depressions to prevent the formation of tide lines. Never submerge an object if you are uncertain how it was made or what it is made of.

Storage

Do not store glass or ceramics near high heat sources such as fireplaces, radiators, or heat vents. Ceramics and glass should not be stored in areas of frequent or significant temperature fluctuations such as attics, unfinished basements, or barns.

If items are to be stored for a prolonged period, they should be protected from dust in boxes, or you can make protective enclosures or covers from Tyvek or Milenex. Never place ceramics directly on shelves or in boxes. Artifacts should be placed on polyester felt or acid-free paper or board. Rough feet of some items could catch on polyester felt so use a smoother product such as paper, board, or Tyvek

Thin stemware, goblets, candlesticks, and bowls should be stored with the widest and most stable part of the artifact down. Unstable ceramics and glass should be padded and secured in place with beanbags, rings, or polyester felt. These can be purchased or made (see Appendix 14: Making Padding for Ceramics and Glass Storage). Leave space between the artifacts for handling. When stacking plates, place no more than four to six plates in each stack, and insert padding between each plate.

Seal wooden storage shelves with acrylic latex paint or water-based polyurethane varnish, and allow the shelves to air for at least two weeks after painting before placing artifacts on them. Although ceramics and glass are not particularly sensitive to vapours emitted from enamelled steel shelves, these shelves should be avoided since they affect other artifacts. Ceramic or glass artifacts that have silver, copper, or pewter rims, stoppers, or other additions are more sensitive to the gases emitted by wood, paints, and enamelled steel.

Ceramics and glass stored or displayed should be placed on shelves that have a lip or barrier to prevent the artifacts from tipping and falling. You can make lips and barriers on shelves from a strip of wood or plastic purchased at a hardware store and glued either with a wood glue or a PVA adhesive to the shelf or from a small elastic or cloth band stretched across the front of the shelf.

Barrier stretched 2- 3 cm above the front and side

Lip glued to the front and side edges of the shelf

Diagram 18: Shelf preparation for glass and ceramics

Display

Displaying ceramics and glass in open cases, cabinets, or shelves allows dust to gather on the surface. Enclosed cabinets reduce dust and the need for frequent handling during cleaning. Hangers or stands used to displaying glass and ceramics should not put pressure on the artifact. Do not use tension stands or hangers with springs. Glass and ceramics on display should be secured from tipping by using pads, sticky wax, or display rings.

Never use valuable or irreplaceable artifacts for food or flowers. When using ceramics or glass objects for flowers, place an insert inside to prevent the artifact from absorbing the water or use artificial flowers.

When to Call a Conservator

Never clean a ceramic or glass artifact if the surface is rough or damaged. Do not clean ceramics if you are uncertain what it is or how it was made. If there are metallic embellishments or if paint is applied over the glaze layer, cleaning should be referred to a conservator. Problems in the decorative layer or glaze should always be referred to a conservator.

Breaks

Broken or chipped glass or ceramic artifacts should be referred to a conservator. Save all the pieces, no matter how small. If the pieces are properly stored in a box with interleafing so they cannot rub together, the repair can be done at any time in the future. Never attempt a repair at home. Re-firing, though often attempted, is not a viable means of repair. Reheating of ceramics to these temperatures often causes greater damage such as pits or holes in the surface or an explosion of the body and burning. If reheating is suggested as a repair method, seek a second opinion.

CHAPTER 11

Silver, Coins, and Medals

Damage to metal artifacts can most frequently be attributed to poor environmental conditions or poor handling. Since metals are highly reactive to the environment, it is best to maintain stable conditions. Even if the environmental conditions cannot be completely controlled, metals can be protected with the proper coatings and enclosures.

Moisture is the most serious environmental hazard. Increased humidity increases the rate of tarnishing. A relative humidity of 55 percent or lower is recommended.

Other common damages to metal artifacts can be attributed to poor handling, cleaning, storage, or display. Mechanical damage includes cracks, dents, pitting, abrasion, separation or loss of applied surfaces from the base layer, and disruption (visible change) of the intended surface finish.

It is essential that you handle all metals wearing gloves to prevent fingerprinting. Salts and oils can mark silver, increase tarnishing, and etch the surface.

Silver

Not all silver is what it appears to be. There are many kinds of silver plate and white metal alloys that look very similar to sterling silver. Some artifacts that appear to be silver are really made from other metals. "Silver" refers to a piece made of solid silver. Solid silver pieces are labelled "sterling" in Canada and the United States. In Britain, solid silver is required to have a hallmark. Hallmarks are published to help you identify and date your silver.

Sheffield plate is a form of inexpensive silverware that was manufactured until the mid-nineteenth century. Sheffield plate was made by bonding a thin layer of silver to a copper support. The copper–silver laminate was then worked like solid silver. Often when pieces of Sheffield plate are joined into complex structures, the copper base is visible at the join. After the mid-nineteenth century, Sheffield plate was slowly replaced by electroplated artifacts, which are cheaper to produce. Electroplated silver artifacts can be produced by electroplating a thin layer of silver to the surface of many different base metals. Plated silver markings can easily be confused with hallmarks. There are several online encyclopedias of international hallmarks and silver plate trademarks to help with identification of silver artifacts. Here are a few:

American Silver Plate Marks
www.silvercollection.it/Americansilverplatemarks.html
British Silver Marks
www.925-1000.com/enyc_Overview.html
British Silver Plate Hallmarks
www.silvercollection.it/SILVERPLATEHALLMARKS.html

Some silver turns out not to be silver at all. In the nineteenth century, many white metal alloys were developed to look like silver but to be more durable and cheaper. One of the most common of those is what is referred to as "nickel silver," which was sold under a variety of trade names. Nickel silver does not contain any silver but is an alloy of zinc, copper, and nickel. It does not have the same lustre as silver, and it will not tarnish.

Silver tarnishes. It is an unavoidable and constant chemical reaction that is difficult to control. Tarnish is silver sulphide, a chemical compound formed when the silver comes in contact with sulphur-containing compounds and gases such as air pollution from car exhausts or gases released from foods, fabrics, and plants. As tarnish forms, artifacts lose part of their lustre, and, as tarnish is removed by cleaning and/or polishing, some of the surface silver is removed as well.

Preservation of Silver

Cleaning, Polishing, and Sealing

Clean silver by first removing surface dust and particle accumulation with a soft cloth or distilled water. Never wet silver artifacts with any other component materials like wood, bone, ivory or felt pads.

Polishing silver removes some of the surface silver of the artifact so polishing should be done infrequently. It is important when polishing any metal to be diligent in the removal of all cleaning products and polishing residues. Do not use multi-metal polishes; these are often more abrasive than polishes specifically produced for silver. Choose a **polish** that will not scratch. Try the polish on a piece of Plexiglas or other acrylic laminate first to assure that it will not scratch. As polish ages, it becomes dryer and more abrasive. If a polish has not been used for a while, dispose of it safely and purchase fresh polish. Excessive polishing can wear down hallmarks and the edges of incised decorations, making them difficult to read. Polishing silver plate can reveal the under-lying metal support and cause a splotched and uneven looking surface.

Never polish silver that has a lacquer applied to the surface. If the lacquer is cracked or flaking, contact a conservator.

Silver dips are highly acidic, which allows them to remove tarnish quickly, but also remove a larger amount of the surface silver than polish. If the dipping solvent is not thoroughly removed, the residue will damage the surface of the silver. This is a particular problem with vessels and highly ornate works with deep crevasses. Many silver dips contain the carcinogen, thiourea. Silver dips are not recommend and should never be used on silver plate as they will quickly remove the silver surface layer, revealing the base metal.

To maintain a polished surface or to remove minimal tarnish, use a silver cloth. Silver cloths are impregnated with polishing material that is less abrasive than pastes, liquids, or foam polishes since the polish is distributed through the fabric and somewhat "padded" by the fibres.

Formulas for polishes do change. It is good to check with a conservator about any possible changes to a polish formula or newly available products.

Currently recommended polishes and cloths:

- Twinkle Anti-Tarnish Silver Polish
- Goddard's Long Term Silver Foam
- Gorham Silver Polishing Cloth
- Hagerty Silver Gloves with R-22 that maintains polished surfaces
- Birks' Anti-Tarnish Silver Polish Cloth

Galvanic cleaning (with aluminum foil and washing soda) can quickly strip electroplated silver from the base metal and leave solid silver without lustre, making the artifact susceptible to tarnishing again quickly. It also can cause pitting of the surface.

Storage and Display

When preparing a silver artifact for storage, it should be lightly buffed to remove any oils, prints, or marks. The rate of tarnish can be slowed by wrapping silver in acid-free non-buffered, anti-tarnish tissue or silver cloth. After wrapping in tissue or a silver cloth, enclose the artifact in a polyethylene bag sealed with tape to reduce contact with high levels of relative humidity.

Never wrap silver in common kitchen cling wrap. These plastics hold in moisture that advances the tarnish and marks your object where the wrap is in tight contact. These heavy tarnish marks are hard to reduce and/or remove.

Other Metals

Pewter and Britannia (modern pewter) are silver in colour and can be confused with silver. These metals do not have the lustre of silver and they grey with time. These metals are softer than silver and should never be polished. Over time, they will form a grey **patina** or surface coating that should not be removed.

Copper-alloy objects are generally allowed to naturally develop a patina. Removing surface grime, dust, and grease (usually from fingerprints) can greatly improve the appearance of an artifact.

When to Call a Conservator

Silver that has a patchy or uneven surface appearance can be electroplated silver that is separating from the base metal — called plate peel. Another possibility is that the silver plate or sterling had a previously applied lacquer coating that has worn away unevenly. Lacquer layers that are disturbed, cracked, or worn tarnish rapidly, which can permanently disfigure the surface. A conservator should remove the applied lacquer, especially if the artifact is a composite piece including wood, bone, ivory, or other materials, such as combs, brushes, mirrors, that could be damaged by the solvents. The colour of a lacquer coating can shift with time turning yellow.

A conservator should apply protective lacquer coatings or wax. If the lacquer or wax coating is not properly and evenly applied, the effort can result in uneven tarnishing and damage to the artifact, especially if it is composed of more than one material.

Hire a conservator to clean previously buried archaeological metals.

Iron and steel corrosion is one of the most complicated problems faced by object conservators, and cleaning and treatment of these items should always be referred to a conservator.

Re-plating of a silver plate artifact is never recommended. It is tempting to make it look nice, but it can actually lower the value, especially of Sheffield plate pieces.

Coins and Medals (Awards)

Coins should only be handled when necessary. Hold them by their edges. Always wear clean white cotton gloves. Fingerprints can easily etch onto the surface of a coin disrupting the surface and lowering its value.

Cleaning

Proofs and non-circulated coins should only be cleaned by a conservator or coin specialist. Cleaning can reduce the value of a coin, especially proof coins. Proof coins are often characterized by a bright mirror-like surface with a "frosted" design. The abrasion that occurs during cleaning can damage the intended contrast between the two surfaces. The natural change in patina and colouring should not be altered. Copper proof coins might have black spots on the surface. These "carbon spots" generally cannot be removed.

Collections of circulated coins should be cleaned to remove surface dirt, grime, and oily residue from handling. Light cleaning will improve the long-term preservation of previously circulated coins. Wash the coins in lukewarm water with a mild soap and a soft brush. Remove only the surface dirt and not the underlying patina. *Do not scrub!*

Rinse with distilled water and degrease by soaking in alcohol or pure acetone for a few minutes (it is not recommended that you use fingernail polish remover). Pure solvents (acetone, or alcohols such as ethanol or iso-propanol) can be purchased in small quantities from most paint or hardware stores. The degreasing should be done in a very well ventilated area,

Even coins that do not appear to be greasy should be degreased to remove any oils, salt, or moisture from handling. After degreasing, they should be air dried for several hours prior to packing for storage.

Medals and Awards

Most military medals were issued with a bright surface and should be maintained that way. You should always wear clean, white cotton gloves when handling medals and awards to prevent the transfer of oils and salt from your hands that will damage the surface.

The various components of medals and awards make them difficult to clean. Lightly tarnished medals can be cleaned with a polishing cloth. It is important to protect any ribbons or other components by temporarily covering them with plastic wrap. Tarnish is easily transferred during handling and can stain the ribbons. Heavily tarnished medals with component materials should be referred to a conservator.

Some medals, such as the Victoria Cross, are issued with a patina that should not be disturbed. Other medals are painted with enamel that can become damaged with handing or poor environmental conditions, especially rapid and large humidity fluctuations of more than 10 degrees within a few hours.

Commemorative medals and academic achievement award medals issued without ribbons or other component materials should be treated the same way as coins.

Storage and Display

When storing and displaying coins and medals, it is important to maintain a low relative humidity. Light can damage ribbons and other component materials but does not affect metal. Ribbons and fabrics should be exposed to no more than 50 lux of light.

Coins and medals should always be stored within protective enclosures. Do not use paper envelopes; paper will abrade the surface. Clear plastic pouches or polyvinyl chloride pouches are not recommend for long-term storage as they can trap moisture and cause deterioration of the surface finish. For long term storage of coins, use coin protectors made from a folded square of acid-free cardboard with a Melinex (polyester plastic) window.

The coin is inserted into the centre of the window and the two sides of the card are stapled together.

Medals are often awarded or presented in boxes or small cases. You should keep them.

Wooden storage cabinets, shelves, or boxes should be avoided when storing or displaying coins and metals. Security is an issue and displaying valuable coins and medals should be done with great caution and with theft prevention in mind.

When to Call a Conservator

It is important to consult a conservator prior to cleaning or storage if it is unclear whether a coin has been circulated or is a proof. If you are not sure if a coin's surface has a patina or surface grime, consult a conservator for cleaning. If there is any uncertainty whether a coin or medal should be cleaned or what the appropriate cleaning method or the extent of cleaning required might be, consult a conservator. If medals have several component materials, again, you might consult a conservator about cleaning or storage. A conservator can resolve storage issues concerning the compatibility of presentation boxes and the long-term preservation of coins and medals.

CHAPTER 12

Digital Media

The long-term preservation of digital media is a problem. A Harris Interactive study sponsored by Seagate Technology[1] found that only about 46 percent of the public regularly back up their data to external devices. When preparing digital media materials for storage, never use rewritable disks and do not use stickers or adhesive labels on the disks for identification. Humidity, light, and heat can all cause deterioration of digital data media storage materials.

However, most data is lost due to technological advances. Data is lost as the media on which it is stored becomes obsolete. As software advances and hardware is replaced, the data becomes unreadable or inaccessible. As technology advances, it is important to save all your information, photographs, and other data in a format that can be easily read and has not become outdated.

It is best to back up your data onto an external hard drive. Make more than one copy of your files and store the copies in various locations — your office, home, and a safety deposit box, for example — to improve the possibility of long-term preservation and protect against loss due to disaster.

1. "Seagate Teams with Microsoft to Promote Backup," International Consumer Electronics Show, Scotts Valley, California, 2007.

Most digital photography is dependent on both specific hardware and software. Digital photograph files must be converted regularly to into a storage format that can easily be transferred. There are websites that will save your images but these sites do not replace the need for you to maintain your own copies of the images. Printing images with archival inks and papers will also help to preserve your photographs. Electronic mail and files should all be saved as simple text files or printed. Additional tips and information about the long term care and preservation of digital media may be found on the U.S. Library of Congress website Preserving Your Digital Memories.

Preservation of family documents, books, artwork, collections and other artifacts allow pieces of history to be passed down from generation to generation. Many basic preservation techniques have been explained with additional information, references, suppliers, and resources listed in the appendixes. Conservation, restoration, and preservation allow us to enjoy and learn from art and artifacts for years to come.

APPENDIX I

Accession List Information

An accession record should include the following information about the artifact:

- title and description
- date or period of fabrication
- date received
- measurements of the object
- artist or maker (if known)
- inventory or tracking number (if applicable)
- how the artifact was acquired (purchase, gift, bequest, etc.)
- purchase price or appraisal value (if known)
- insurance information (if applicable)

Additional information might include the following:

- marks, labels, or seals
- medium or materials of construction
- photograph of the artifact
- condition or conservation notes
- publication references

- history of the object
- location within your home
- who should receive the object after the death of the present owner

ITEM: 103

TITLE/DESCRIPTION: Wedding Certificate. Thought to be vellum. Printed with information filled in with ink (probably a fountain pen)

DATE OF FABRICATION: Fay Louise Spurlock 27 May 1908 Halifax, NS, when she married Dr. John Henry Schaefer. (Printed portion predates completed certificate.)

MAKER:

RECEIVED as bequest upon her death 30 April 1983

MEASUREMENTS: Height 29 ½ cm width 54 cm

NOTES: Unframed, received rolled and flattened. Deformations from plane, the document will not lay flat. Some staining, possibly from water, in the upper left corner which repeats every 8 cm across the top edge showing that damage occurred while rolled.

APPENDIX 2

How to Find and Choose a Conservation Professional

There are several ways to find a professional conservator. You might obtain referrals from conservation organizations such as the Canadian Conservation Institute (CCI), Canadian Association of Professional Conservators (CAPAC-ACRP), Conservation Association for Cultural Property (CAC-ACCR), other conservation professionals, collectors, galleries, or local museums.

You should contact at least three conservators and ask about the following:

- training
- experience
- scope of practice: type of objects treated and other activities undertaken
- affiliation with conservation organizations
- availability
- references

The quality of conservation work should be based on the technical and structural work of the treatment in additional to the cosmetic appearance. References from museum and other conservation professionals can help with this evaluation.

Once you find a conservator, the procedure for contracting treatment may vary slightly but usually consists of bringing the object in question to the conservation professional and leaving it for a complete examination and the development of a treatment plan. There may be a charge for this initial examination, either a flat rate or an hourly rate, which might include a provision for additional examinations and procedures, such as un-framing, disassembly, chemical analysis, or X-rays.

Before you leave your object with the conservator for examination or treatment you should discuss and feel comfortable with the following:

- Ensure that there is an adequate level of reversibility to the materials to be used during treatment of your artifact.
- What degree of aesthetic restoration is desired?
- Will your artifact be prepared for storage or display after treatment?
- What will be the format of reports, documentation, photographs (minimally you should ask for before and after treatment photo-documentation of your object), and notification of any changes to the treatment plan?
- Cost?
- Timeline?
- Who will insure your artifact while it is in the possession of the conservator?

Once the initial examination is complete and the treatment proposal and cost are determined, a contract should be prepared to reflect the findings and the amount of time expected to complete the treatment. Often, half the payment is requested at this time along with a complete materials cost.

Please note that conservation treatments are often tedious and time consuming due to the nature of the procedures and are hardly ever done as quickly as you would like, but the conservator should keep you informed in writing of any significant change in the estimated time of completion.

After treatment of your object is complete, you should be given a dossier of documentation that should include the initial examination and statement of the pre-treatment condition of the object, the proposed treatment plan, and the actual treatment plan with a list of materials used for the treatment procedures. Photo-documentation of the treatment should include at least one image of before and after treatment. Additional images may be included depending on the complexity of the procedures, especially if there is to be significant reintegration of damaged areas, if there was structural damage, or if there has been aesthetic restoration.

Conservation Organizations

Canadian Conservation Institute-
Institut Canadien de Conservation (CCI-l'ICC)
1030 Innes Road
Ottawa, ON K1A 0M5
(613) 998-3721
1-866-998-3721
www.cc1-icc.gc.ca

Canadian Association of Professional Conservators-
Association Candienne des restaurateurs professionnels
(CAPC-ACRP)
c/o Canadian Museums Association
Suite 400, 280 Metcalf St.
Ottawa, ON K2P 1R7
greg-hill@pch.gc.ca

Conservation Association for Conservation-
Association Canadienne pour la Conservation et la Restauration
(CAC-ACCR)
207 Bank Street, Suite 419
Ottawa, ON K2P 2N2
(613) 231-3977

American Institute for Conservation of
Historic and Artistic Works
1156 15th Street NW Suite 320
Washington DC 20005-1714
info@aic-faic.org

APPENDIX 3

Using a Camera to Measure Approximate Light Levels

To measure lux, set the ASA/ISO at 800 and the shutter speed at 1/60. Aim the single reflex camera camera (SRL) at a white board in front of the artifact and adjust the aperture to the correct exposure (done automatically on many cameras). This will give you the approximate number of lux.

f 4 = 50 lux
f 5.6 = 100 lux
f 8 = 200 lux
f 11= 400 lux
f 16 = 800 lux

Some advanced digital cameras allow this type of measurement (also known as "setting the white balance") but you may not be able to take a light reading this way with a basic digital camera. Light meters (photometers) to measure lux are available, or you can use a photography light meter following the instructions for direct rather than reflective light.

Adapted from CCI Note 2/5 *Using a Camera to Measure Light Levels* (Canadian Conservation Institute, Ottawa, ON, 1992).

APPENDIX 4

General Rules for Handling and Moving Artifacts and Works of Art

A great deal of damage can occur in a very short amount of time simply through human error and mishandling. Here are some guidelines for handling your family treasures.

The most important rule when handling an artifact is *never* have or use pens or ink *anywhere* near an artifact, not even in your pocket! If you have to write while near an artifact, use a pencil.

General Procedures for Handling all Artifacts

1. Know where an object will be moved prior to picking it up and make sure the space is adequate for the object.
2. Prior to moving an object, check that there are no loose or moving parts. If parts are made to be separated (like pendulums of clocks or drawers of a desk) remove them from the object and move them separately to avoid damage. If pieces move but are not removable (for example, the drop leaves of a table) secure them with soft cloth ropes (not tape) so they will not be harmed and will not damage the primary structure.

3. Never try to move an object that is either too heavy or large to manage easily.
4. Never walk backwards while carrying an object unless guided.
5. Wear clean cotton gloves when carrying works or art (except heavily glazed ceramics, glass, or other smooth slippery surfaces).
6. Handle only one object at a time no matter how small.
7. Use two hands when moving an object no matter how small.
8. Never drag an object: if it is too heavy to lift, find additional handlers.
9. Never leave works directly on the floor.
10. Never discard packing materials before searching them for pieces that may have separated during transit.
11. Take your time and move slowly.

Unframed Works of Art on Paper, Parchment, or Vellum

Mounted and Matted Artifacts

1. Mounted and matted items with a rigid or semi-rigid support should only be handled by the supporting materials. Never touch the artifact.
2. Always keep mounted and matted works face up and flat. Placing items face down may result in their separating from the mount or matt package, and artifacts can slip through or get caught on the edge of the matt window, causing tearing.
3. Stack only works of similar size and shape together with the largest on the bottom.

4. If items are matted and one corner of all items is aligned, no matt openings should be visible.
5. Keep stacks shallow and limit the number of items on them.

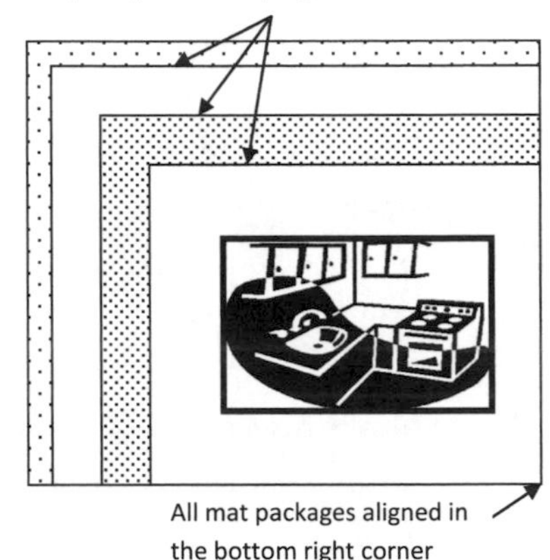

Diagram 19:
Stacking matted works

Unmounted and Unmatted Artifacts

1. Lift loose sheets by the upper corners so that they hang freely without bending or buckling. Do not carry them in this manner as air currents can cause creasing. Place sheets on a sheet of clean cardboard (preferably acid-free) to move them.
2. Lay works on a clean and level surface.
3. Works produced with easily smudged materials such as charcoal or pastels should be carried separately and never stacked.
4. If you must stack un-mounted works (never recommended but sometimes unavoidable), always separate works with separation sheets such as **glassine**.

5. Never move stacked work (mounted, matted, or unmounted) unless they are stacked within a Solander box or other supporting box. The box should be kept flat and level when being moved.

Books

1. Books should be stored on a shelf upright, by size, tallest to shortest.
2. Always support books with bookends.
3. Do not pack books too tightly on shelves. Allow for some air circulation.
4. When removing books from a shelf, grasp the middle of the spine and pull gently. Never pull from the head cap (the small turn over of the binding at the top and bottom of the spine).
5. When moving heavy or damaged volumes use both hands and carry the volume in the horizontal position.
6. Large volumes may be placed horizontally on a shelf. Keep stacked volumes to a minimum.
7. Never place objects such as paper clips, papers, or flowers and leaves in books.
8. Never place a rubber band around a book.

Paintings and Framed Works

1. Before picking up a framed work, make sure the artifact is secure in the frame.
2. Wear gloves.

3. Only handle the work by the frame. Do not touch the back or front of the artifact.
4. Before picking up the object, make sure your path is clear and all doors are open.
5. Never rest another object on or against the front or back surfaces of the artifact.
6. Framed works should be handled with two hands. One hand supports the bottom of the frame and one is placed on the side of the frame.
7. If the painting is large or heavy, ask for help. Never drag a framed work — that can cause damage and loosen the corners of the frame.
8. Never insert your fingers between the stretcher and the canvas.
9. If the frame is ornate or gilded, use latex gloves. Cotton gloves can catch on the gesso and pull off ornaments or the surface finish.
10. Never rest a framed work on its corner.
11. Never rest a framed work on the ground and balance it with one hand. It is better to lean it against a secure surface like a wall.
12. Framed works should be stored vertically, never laid flat.
13. If paintings must be stacked temporarily, never stack framed works with unframed works.
14. Padding should be placed beneath frames temporarily stacked or leaned against a wall to prevent skidding and protect the frame.
15. When stacking, never stack works together that are not of a comparable size. It is important that the front and the back of the artifact not be touched by the next item, frame to frame. If items are not close in size insert a

piece of cardboard that is larger than the largest frame between the artifacts.

16. If the framing hardware, such as screw-eyes, protrudes, the frames should not be stacked.
17. When stacking frames, they should be oriented face-to-face, back-to-back.
18. Keep the number of items stacked together to a minimum.

Textiles

1. Always wash your hands first.
2. Remove all jewellery and do not wear shirts, blouses, or jackets that have buttons, zippers, or hooks that can catch on the textile threads or fibres.
3. Wear white cotton gloves. Gloves will help reduce the transfer to the textiles of oils that occur naturally on your skin. White will help you see any dye transfer or flaking of decoration or fibres.
4. Prepare a space sufficient to lay the textile flat with no folding, bunching, or creasing. Clean it thoroughly and lay out a clean cotton sheet or acid-free paper to place the textile upon (old cotton mattress pads are excellent for this purpose).
5. When moving small textiles, always support the object with a rigid piece of cardboard.
6. If you must turn a fragile textile over, sandwich the object between two pieces of cardboard and flip the sandwich.
7. Large flat textiles should be moved on a board or rolled on a tube. If placed on a board. The textile should be folded as few times as possible to fit safely on the support

board and with each fold stuffed with tissue or muslin to prevent creasing.

8. Three dimensional textiles and costumes (clothing) should be moved on a board whenever possible or in a box. If the textile is strong enough and is usually stored on a hanger, you can use the hanger to move the piece.
9. Never lift a textile by the border or edge.
10. Try to keep folding and unfolding to a minimum.

Sculpture, Ceramics, Glass, Baskets, and Metal Artifacts

1. Unglazed ceramics should be handled with gloves. If the surface is rough, wear latex gloves.
2. Glazed ceramics and glass should be handled with clean dry hands only. *Do not wear gloves* because items can easily slip.
3. Lift objects by sliding one hand underneath while the other hand is used to steady the object.
4. Never lift by the edge, lip, or handle (even if designed for carrying, the handle is often one of the weakest parts of the construction).
5. When transporting items, place them on their most stable edge. For example, a bowl is often wider at the brim and would be more stable brim down.
6. Never lift a sculpture by a protruding part such as a leg, arm, head, etc.
7. Never touch metals with your bare hands. The oils and salt from your hands promote corrosion.
8. Touch stone sculptures with clean hands.

Furniture

1. Remove marble or glass furniture tops. These tops should be moved vertically.
2. Secure any leaves or other hinged parts with soft ties.
3. Remove or secure drawers with soft ties.
4. Never drag furniture. That can damage or break the legs.
5. Do not lift by the arms or other protrusions. Lift by the most structurally secure area, like the seat of a chair.
6. Do not store, transport, or display furniture in any orientation other than its intended construction (for example, tilted upside-down). The piece is not constructed to take the stress or weight of the object in these orientations.

APPENDIX 5

Encapsulation Process

Materials and Supplies List

- cotton gloves
- air bulb or compressed air (available from photo supply stores)
- lint-free microfibre cleaning cloth (found at grocery stores and hardware stores)
- Melinex pre-cut standard sheet or roll: 3, 4, or 5 mil thicknesses
- 3M 415 double-sided tape (various thicknesses are available but ¼ in to ½ in is usually adequate)
- self-healing cutting mat or grid graph paper
- bone folder
- scissors
- ruler
- weight (a bean bag, small smooth bottomed container filled with rice, etc.)

1. Prepare your work area by cleaning it thoroughly with a lint-free microfibre cloth or by spraying the work space

with compressed air. Melinex polyester film is static charged and attracts dust. Working on a self-healing cutting board or over a piece of grid graph paper will help to align the two layers of Melinex, the artifact, and the double-sided tape.

2. Place a Melinex sheet at least 2 cm larger than the artifact on the work surface and wipe with the lint-free cloth.
3. Next, place your artifact in the centre of the Melinex, aligning it with the grid lines on your paper or board so it is centred, and place a small weight on the centre of the artifact to hold it in place while you lay the double-sided tape.
4. Leave the released paper on the 3M 415 double-sided tape. Lay the adhesive tape at least ⅛ in (5 mm) from the edge of the artifact on all four sides. The tape should not overlap at the corners so there is small space for air exchange.

   *Note: When encapsulating pamphlets lay the tape on only *three* sides so one side remains open for easy access.
5. Remove the released paper from the double-sided tape.
6. Remove the weight from the centre of the artifact.

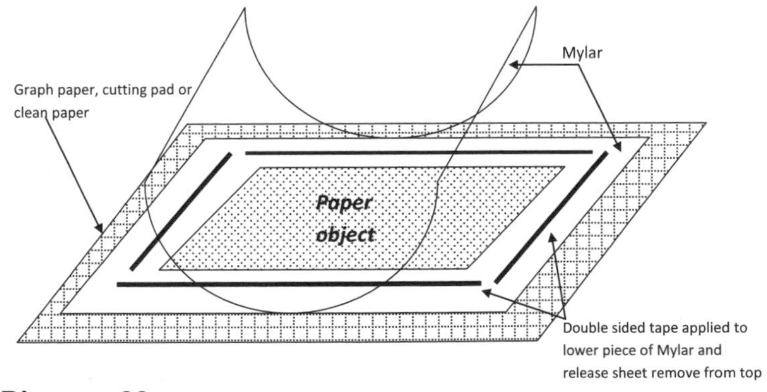

Diagram 20 :
Encapsulation

7. Holding the Melinex in a downward curved fashion align the sheet in the centre of the artifact and lay the sheet over the artifact with a downward sideways pressure to prevent bubbling or creasing of the upper sheet.
8. Cut away excess Melinex if necessary leaving at least 1 cm between the edge of the tape and the exterior edge of the polyester sheet. You can cut Melinex to a standard size to facilitate storage.

APPENDIX 6

Surface Cleaning Books

Materials and Supplies List

- cotton gloves
- soft bristled brush (shaving brushes work well)
- compressed air (available from photo supply stores) or a vacuum cleaner with brush attachment
- lint-free microfibre cleaning cloth (found at grocery stores and hardware stores)
- powder erasers (Scum-X or document cleaning pads)
- solid erasers (vinyl or art gum)

Note: Do *not* clean rough cowhide or suede with erasers and *never* apply moisture when surface cleaning.

1. Wear cotton gloves to prevent the transfer of oils from your skin to the binding or paper.
2. Pass gently over the book with a lint-free cloth to lift any loose particles of dirt.
3. Always test your cleaning method and materials on a small, discrete area before attempting an overall cleaning

of an artifact, because some cleaning can cause abrasion, damage, or discolouration.

4. Pass over the artifact with powdered easers, such as Skum-X by Dietzgen, or use document cleaning pads that contain a grit free powder inside a soft cloth bag. Use a small circular motion to gently work over the entire surface of the artifact.
5. After an overall cleaning, gently brush away any particles of eraser or loosened dirt to evaluate if additional cleaning is necessary. If residual ingrained dirt or light staining is present, a localized cleaning with solid erasers may be attempted.
6. Test the cleaning with any solid eraser in a small, discrete area before proceeding.
7. White vinyl easers, such as Magic Rub or an art gum eraser, can be used by gently passing over the area to be cleaned in a circular manner.
8. After using any eraser products on an artifact, any particles or loosened dirt should be removed by thoroughly brushing or vacuuming.

APPENDIX 7

Angled Supports for Displaying Books

Materials and Supplies List

- acid-free cardboard or book board: .040 or .050 thickness
- sharp blade utility or art knife
- measuring tape or ruler
- cutting mat (optional)
- metal straight edge or T-square
- bone folder
- 3M 415 double-sided tape
- cloth (optional)
- acid-free (pH neutral) PVA (polyvinyl acetate) adhesive

When constructing an angled support or cradle for displaying books, you can make one support to use for many books. The slanted support portion of the cradle must always be slightly shorter and narrower than the book. The rest of the support can be made larger to accommodate different volumes.

1. Measure the width of the block to determine the width

of the board. The board should be narrower than the block of the book.

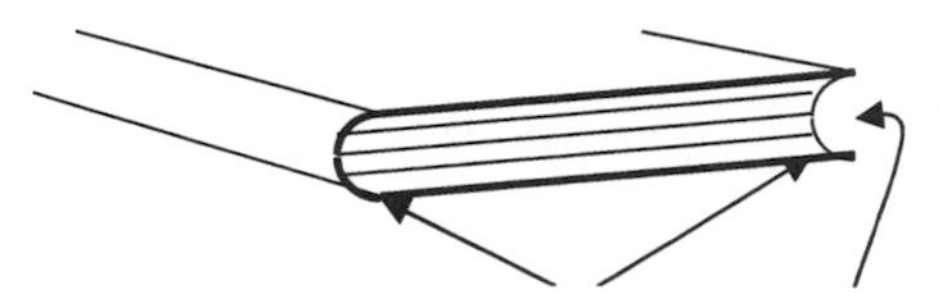

Measure the width and thickness (depth) of the block to determine width of board

Diagram 21:
Taking measurements

2. Cut your board so that the folds will go with the grain. To determine the direction of the grain of the board, flex the board slightly. It will flex more easily with the grain. Another method to determine the direction of the grain is to try and tear the edge. Tearing is easier with the grain.
3. Measure and score fold lines with the bone folder. All folds go in the same direction except the top fold shown in Diagram 22.

Diagram 22:
Measuring the board

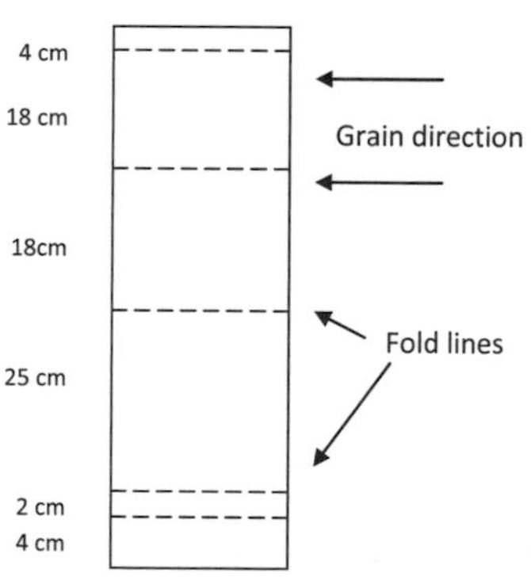

Example measurements for a book

25 H cm x 20 W cm x 3.5 cm thick or smaller

4. Gently fold board in the directions indicated in Diagram 23.

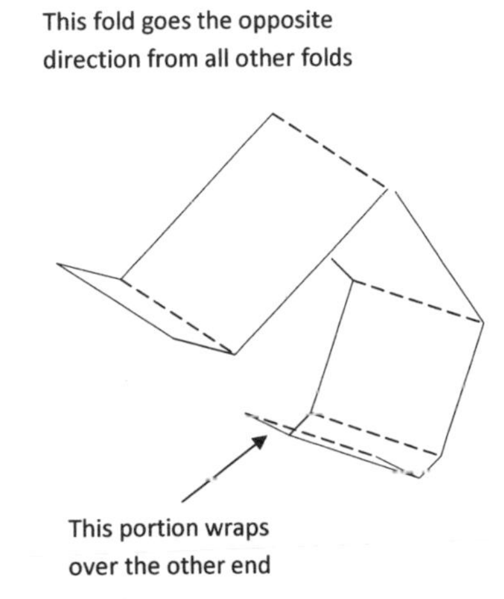

Diagram 23:
Folding the board

5. Secure the portion of the board that wraps over the opposite end using one line of 3M 415 double-sided tape

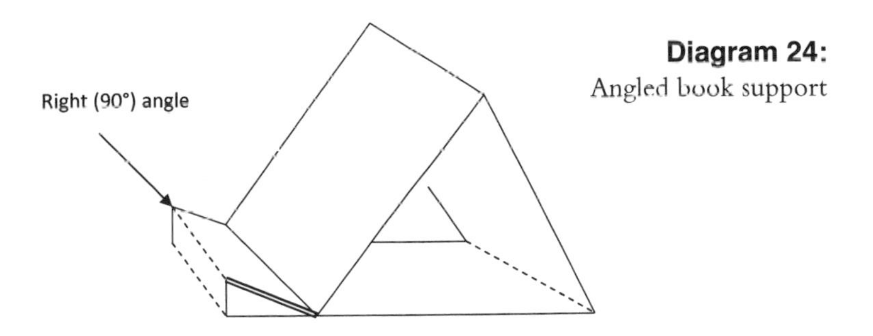

Diagram 24:
Angled book support

*Note: You can cover the support in fabric. Prepare the fabric by washing it at least three times to reduce the risk of dye transfer. Secure the fabric to the underside of the support using 3M 415 double-sided tape or acid-free PVA glue.

APPENDIX 8

Making a Book Cozy

Materials and Supplies List

- quilted cotton fabric with polyester batting
- measuring tape or ruler
- scissors
- thread
- sewing machine (optional)
- twill tape or soft, unbleached cotton ribbon

1. Prepare the fabric by washing it several times to remove any sizing applied during fabrication.

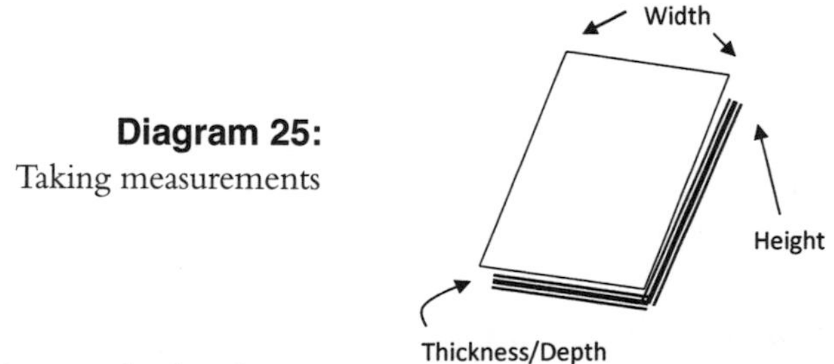

Diagram 25:
Taking measurements

2. Measure the book.
3. Calculate the fabric dimensions and cut the fabric.

Dimension 1: Add height and depth. Dimension 2: Add two times the width plus two times the depth.
Note: it is better to have the final result slightly too big than too small.

4. Cut two pieces of ribbon: one long enough to wrap around the height of the book and be tied (ribbon A); another to wrap around the width the book and be tied (ribbon B).
5. On a sewing machine finish the edges of the fabric using a zigzag stitch or by hand using a blanket stitch, and attach ribbons.

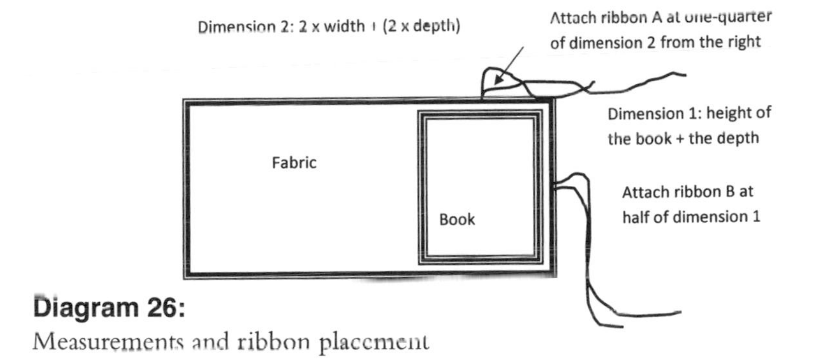

Diagram 26:
Measurements and ribbon placement

*Note: When attaching ribbon A at the top of the cozy the ribbon should not be sewn in the middle. One tail of the ribbon should be much longer to allow it to wrap

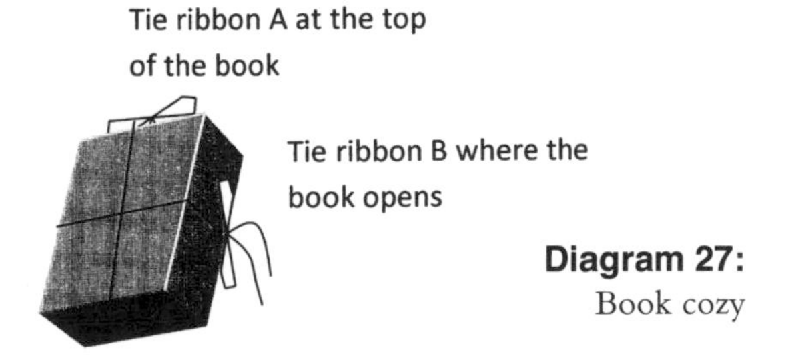

Diagram 27:
Book cozy

APPENDIX 9

Construction of Folders and Book Boxes

all the way around the book before tying.

Materials and Supplies List

- acid-free folder stock, bristle board, or library board
- metal straight edge or T-square
- sharp blade utility knife or art knife
- measuring tape or ruler
- cutting mat (optional)
- bone folder
- acid-free (pH neutral) PVA (polyvinyl acetate) adhesive
- small bowl or plate
- round, stiff bristled paint brush
- two old towels or sheets
- weights (example: heavy pots and pans or phone books on top of a cookie sheet)
- twill tape or soft, unbleached cotton ribbon

1. Measure the book, folio, or pamphlet and complete the worksheet on page 135 to determine the measurements of the boards for the box.

2. After calculating the measurement for the board, cut the board so the folds go in the direction of the grain of the board. To determine the direction of the grain of the board, flex it slightly; it will be easier to flex with the grain. Another method to determine the direction of the grain is to try and tear the edge. Tearing is easier with the grain.
3. Measure and score fold lines with the bone folder on both boards.

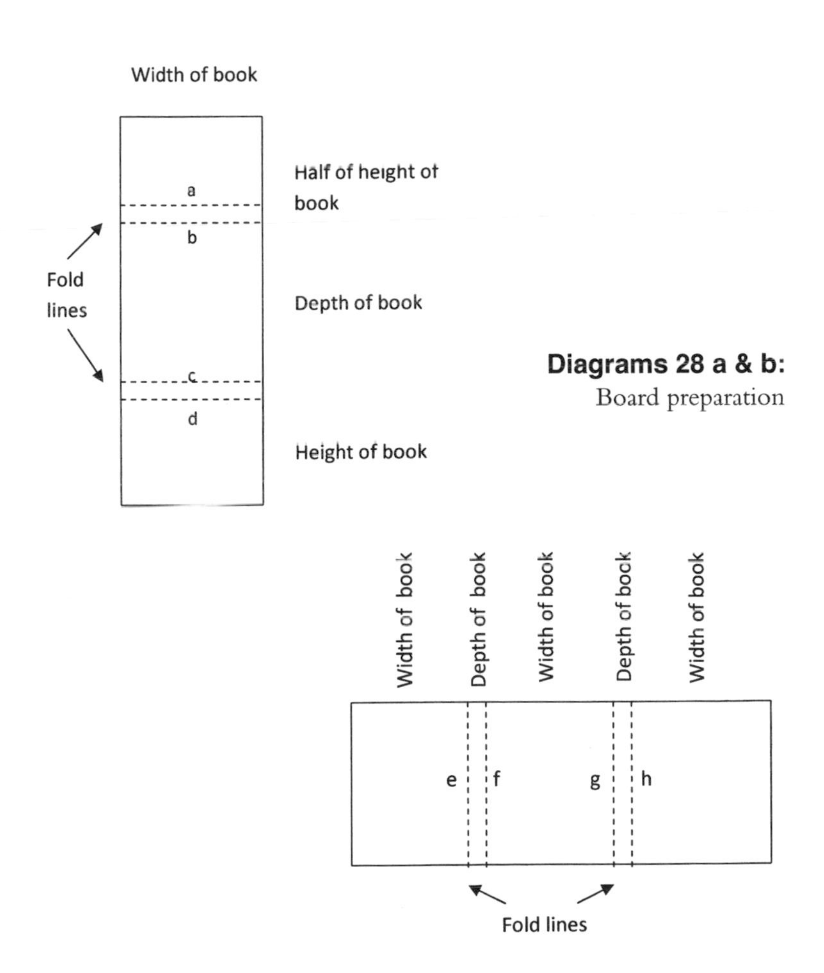

Diagrams 28 a & b:
Board preparation

4. Gently fold the boards.
5. Pour some PVA adhesive into a small plate or bowl.
6. Place board A over an old towel or sheet on a flat work surface.
7. Apply PVA glue in the middle section of board A, using the paint brush in a dabbing motion. Dabbing pushes the adhesive into the fibres of the board creating a stronger bond than brushing the adhesive onto the board.
8. Align the middle section of board B over the glued section of board A.
9. Cover with an old towel or sheet and place weights on top.
10. Allow to dry overnight.
11. Cut two pieces of ribbon long enough to wrap around the width of the book and tie.
12. Cut four small slits in the glued-together section of the boards about 3 cm from each corner.

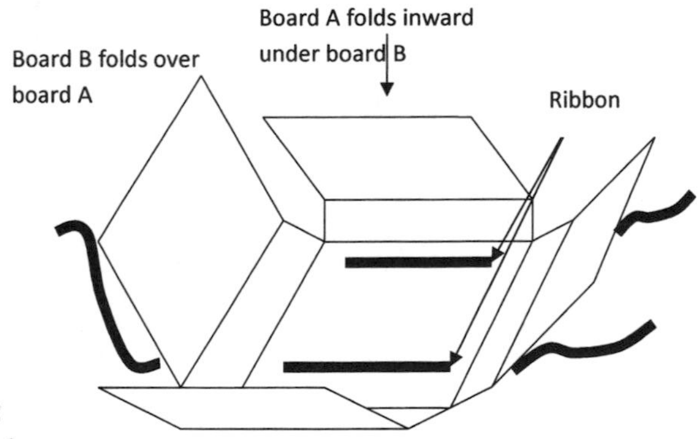

Diagram 29:
Finished book box

13. Starting on the outside of the box (folds all face inward) push the ribbon in and out of the slits as indicated in Diagram 29.
14. Place the book in the box and tie closed.

Worksheet: Calculating Measurements for Book Boxes

Height of Book: ______Width of Book: ______Depth of Book: ______

Measurements Board A:

1. Height of book x 2 =
2. Depth of book x 2 =

Add (1) and (2) to get total length of Board A

Width of Board A= width of book

Measuring the fold lines from the top of the board:

a. Height of book ÷ 2 = ________
b. (a) + depth of book = ________
c. (b) + height of book = ________
d. (c) + depth of book = ________

Measurements Board B:

3. Width of book x 3 =
4. Depth of book x 2 =

Add (3) and (4) to get total width of Board B

Height of Board B = height of book

Measuring the fold lines from the left of the board:

e. Width of book = _______
f. (e) + depth of book = _______
g. (f) + width of book = _______
h. (g) + depth of book = _______

APPENDIX 10

Matting and Framing Paper Artifacts

When framing a work of art or artifact on paper, there are several parts of the frame package to consider. The frame affects the final aesthetics of the work of art and, as long as it is stable and in good condition, it has little effect on the long-term preservation of the artifact.

The artifact is placed into a matt package, which consists of a mounting board and a matt board. The mounting board is the backboard in the package and usually the artifact is attached with hinges to this board. The matt board is the "window" board that goes over the artifact. Choose an acid-free, 100 percent rag, conservation or museum quality board, four-ply thick or thicker. The use of white or buff coloured boards is recommend since many dyes are acidic and, with time, can damage your artifact. Unbuffered boards should be used for albumen, dry transfer, and chromogentic prints, and silk or wool textiles. It is best to choose boards buffered with calcium carbonate. Always confirm that the matt board that will be used for your artifact has passed the **PAT (Photographic Activity Test)**.

The frame should be large enough to accommodate a minimum of 5 cm of matt board on each side of the window.

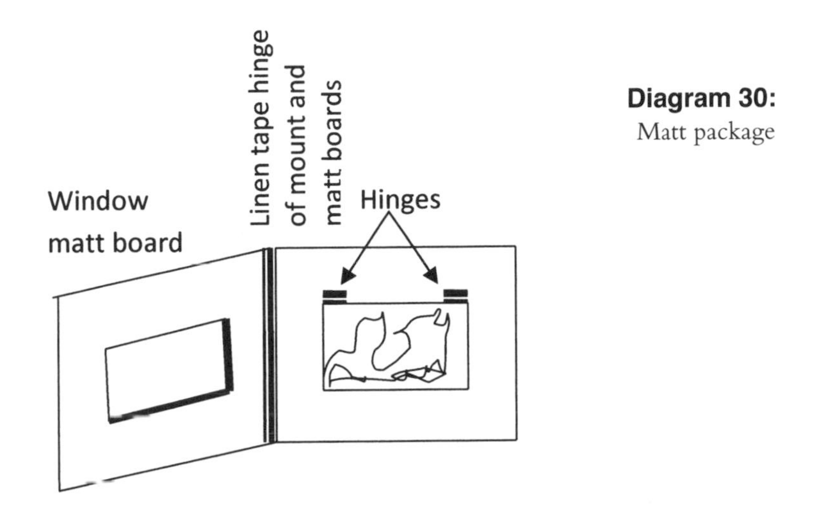

Diagram 30:
Matt package

The matt board and mounting board should be joined together with gummed linen tape. The use of pressure sensitive adhesive tapes is not recommended, but framers often use it.

To secure the artifact in the matt package, it should be hinged using Japanese tissue. There are many gummed and pressure sensitive tapes available from archival suppliers and used by framers. These tapes are often made of inappropriate materials that may degrade and damage your artifact. These tapes are often hard to remove. No tape should be placed around the perimeter of the matt package.

Behind the back mounting board there should be an additional backing board of acid-free material.

There are two primary glazing materials: glass or plastic. Glass is the traditional glazing material and there are three types readily available: window glass, Denglas, and Tru-vue (two types). There are three commonly used plastics: Plexiglass/acrylic (many types), Lucite/Acrylite (several types), and Lexan (two types). Table 5: Glazing Materials and Characteristics illustrates some of the advantages and disadvantages of each product.

Table 5:

Glazing Materials and Characteristics

Characteristics	Denglas	Tru-vue	Window glass	Lucite/Acrylite	Lexan	Plexiglass
Weight	Heavy	Heavy	Heavy but comes in different thicknesses	Lightweight	Lightweight	Lightweight
Static charge	No	No	No	Yes	Yes	Most types
UV absorbers	No	Yes	No	Some types	Yes	Some types
Durability	Reduced breakage due to coating	Breaks	Breaks	Treated to reduce marring	Stronger than plexiglass, resists marring, unbreak-able	Scratches easily
Rigidity and Bowing	Very rigid	Very rigid	Very rigid	Bows easily	Bows easily	Bows easily
Glare reduction	Coated to reduce glare	Conservation clear reduces glare	Textured for glare reduction	No	No	No
Cleaning	Special cleaning recommended	No	No	Special cleaning recommended	Special cleaning recommended	Special cleaning recommended
Cost	Approximately four times window glass	About three times window glass	Cheapest	Double the price of window glass	Between three and four times window glass	Double the price of window glass

The glazing, matt package, and backing board are placed into the frame and secured using framers tip, mending plates, or off-set clips. The framer should not use nails or tacks. The back of the frame should be sealed over the securing hardware to prevent dust and other environmental contaminates from entering the matt package. Frame sealing can be done with linen tape or with an appropriate acid-free, pressure-sensitive, frame sealing tape. Frames should not be sealed with water activated tape, brown paper tape, masking tape, or packing tape.

After the frame package is complete, hanging hardware is secured to the reverse of the frame. Most framers will use screw eyes and picture wire, which loosen with time and can easily be knocked off the wall, or self-levelling bars at the top centre of the frame. Neither method adequately secures frames to the wall. The best way to hang a frame is by applying a D-ring to each vertical side of the reverse of the frame one-third down from the top. Each D-ring is secured to the wall with a picture hanger.

APPENDIX II

Treating Infestations in Textiles by Freezing

You should not treat damp or excessively wet textiles in this manner. Do not pre-cool the textiles by placing them in a cold basement or storage area prior to this treatment. It is very important that the textile go from room temperature directly into the freezer. The freezer should be capable of reaching –20°C. Most stand-alone home freezers are capable of these temperatures while combined freezer/refrigerator units are not.

1. Place the textile in a polyethylene bag and remove excess air by smoothing. Seal the bag with packing tape, a twist tie, or a rubber band.
2. Place only a few articles in the freezer at a time. If you overfill the space, the objects in the middle will not reach freezing temperatures quickly enough to be effective.
3. Objects should be left at –20°C for at least 48 hours.
4. The freezing of the artifacts should be fast but the thawing should be done very slowly. Move the items from the freezer into the refrigerator or other cold storage until thoroughly thawed. Then move them from cold storage to room temperature. Condensation will form on the

outside of the bag but not the inside. Wait until the condensation has completely evaporated and freeze a second time. Thaw in the same manner.

5. After the condensation is completely evaporated, remove the textile from the bag.
6. Clean away any dead insects or larval skins and eggs with a thorough, careful vacuuming. Use tweezers to remove any sticky eggs or larva. Check very carefully in corners, folds, and seams.

Freezing is a disinfectant but not a repellent. If you have textiles that are vulnerable to infestations, it is recommended that they be stored in a loose polyethylene bag.

APPENDIX 12

How to Make a Padded Hanger

Materials

- prepare muslin or cotton sheeting by washing and drying at least three times, the last washing without soap or detergent, and air dry
- polyester batting (available at craft and sewing stores)
- needle and cotton thread

Hangers

Remember that the materials used to manufacture hangers can all damage textiles: wood is acidic, metal oxidizes, and many plastics cause staining and accelerate chemical deterioration of the fibres. Choose the hanger that will best support the clothing; the padding will isolate the textile from the harmful materials.

Single-bar hangers (often plastic or wood) or hangers with inclined shoulder (often for suits)

1. Cover the hanger with a thick layer of polyester batting.
2. Cut a rectangle of muslin or sheeting. Then cut a small hole in the centre. The fabric should be slightly wider than the hanger and large enough to be folded over the hanger and cover all the batting, with a small hole in the centre.
3. Place the hole over the neck of hanger, whipstitch the muslin in place, and allow it to hang freely.

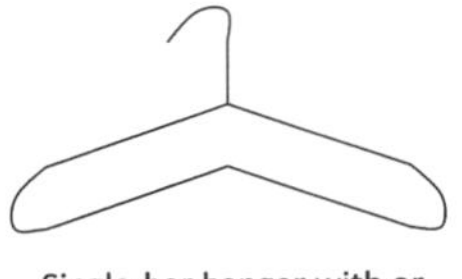

Single-bar hanger with or without shoulder incline

Step 1: Cover with batting

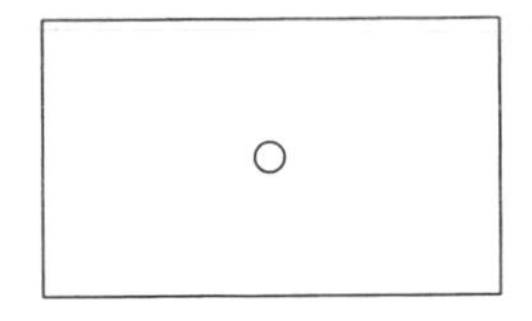

Step 2: Cut muslin with a small hole in the centre

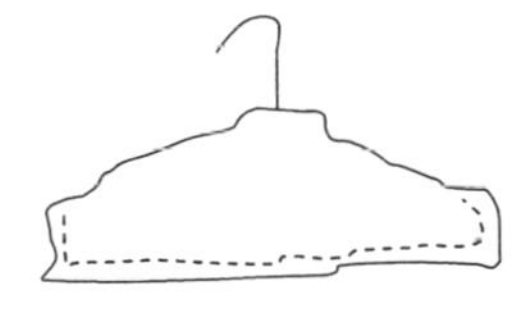

Step 3: Whipstitch the fabric in place

Diagram 31:
Single-bar hangers

Metal Hangers

Treated metal hangers the same as single-bar hangers except you need to cover them with sufficient polyester batting to cover both the upper and lower metal wires of the hanger.

Bend metal hanger prior to padding to accommodate children's clothes.

Diagram 32:
Metal hangers

Straight Pant and Skirt Hangers That Apply Pressure

1. Try to pick a hanger that does not have grooves cut into the wood or plastic.
2. Skirt hangers usually are not as wide as pant hangers.
3. Align the pants or skirt carefully so that the seams are at the sides and straight.
4. Cover the top of the pants or skirts with a layer of muslin or sheeting.
5. Cover the muslin with a layer of polyester batting at least ½ cm thick.
6. Close the hanger assuring that no fabric is extending past the top of the bar and that no creases are caused by the bars.

If an item to be hung needs extra support, sew a piece of twill tape or white grosgrain ribbon into the seam allowance. Then tie the ribbon onto the neck of the hanger.

APPENDIX 13

Boxing Medium to Large Textiles for Storage

Materials

- acid-free boxes (always use the biggest box possible for textile storage)
- acid-free or acid-free buffered tissue (use acid-free buffered tissue for cotton, linen, or other cellulose based fabrics; for all composite textiles or those made of silk, wool, or other protein-based fibres use unbuffered acid-free tissue)
- muslin or cotton sheeting (prepare prior to use by washing and drying at least three times, the last washing without soap or detergent, and air dry)
- polyester batting (available at craft and sewing stores)

Flat Textiles

1. Lay the textile on top of a muslin or cotton sheet spread on a clean, flat surface.
2. Make a padding "sausage" by crumpling tissue or wrapping polyester batting in prepared fabric.
3. Place the "sausage" approximately one-third to one-quarter

from the top of the textile depending on how many times the textile will need to be folded to fit in the box. Fold upper portion of textile over "sausage" roll.

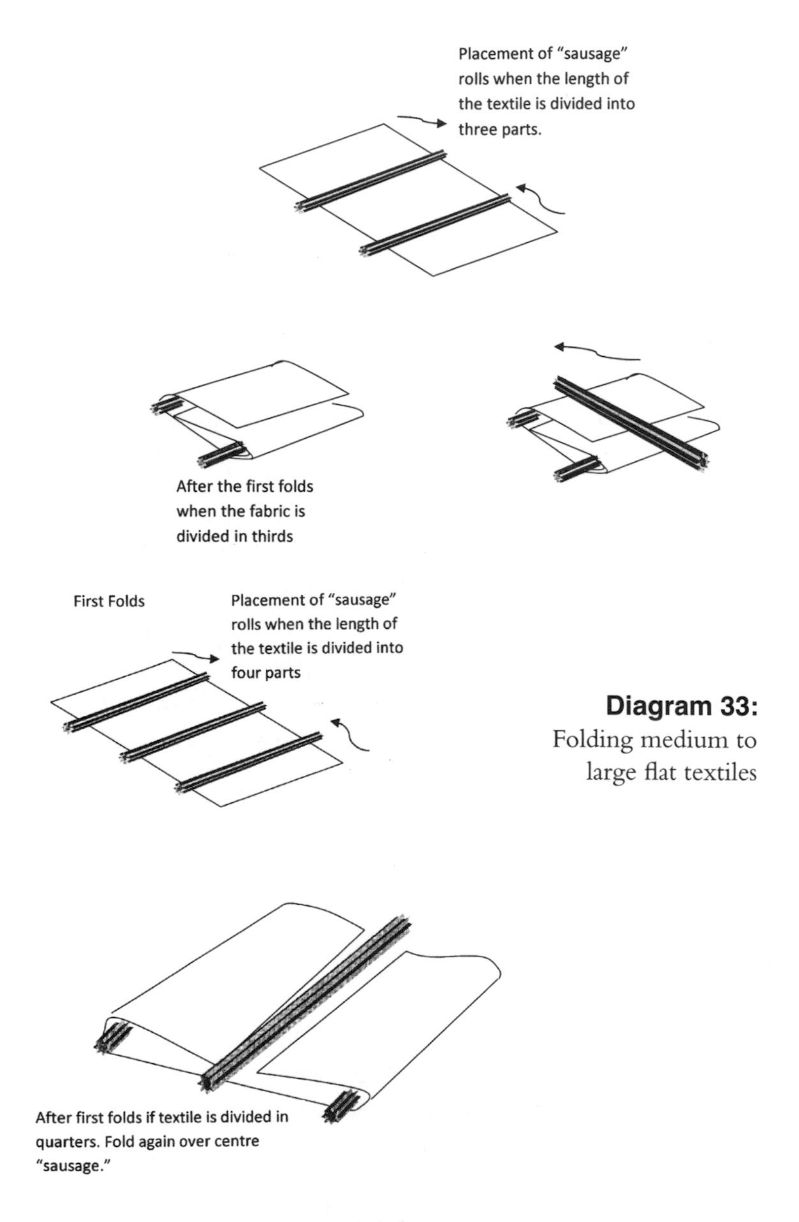

Diagram 33: Folding medium to large flat textiles

4. Place another "sausage" approximately one-third to one-quarter from the bottom of the textile and fold the lower portion of the textile over the "sausage" roll. *Note: if the textile was large enough to require being folded in quarters another "sausage" roll should be place in the middle and the textile folded over the roll.
5. Using the box length, decide how many folds will be required to make the textile fit snugly but without being crumpled or forced to fit.
6. Place "sausage" rolls and fold toward the centre of the textile.
7. After folding the textile, wrap it with cotton, muslin, or tissue and place it into the acid-free box.

Medium to Large Three-dimensional Textiles and Costumes

Most three-dimensional costumes would be best stored hung since the seams were constructed to take stress in this orientation and hanging holds the shape of the piece better.

Medium to large three-dimensional textiles that should be stored boxed are those that have heavily applied ornamentation such as beading, pearls, or sequins, or textiles made of very lightweight or fine fabrics that could distort when hung, such as weighted silks and gauze, and knitted items.

1. Lay the textile on top of a muslin or cotton sheet spread on a clean, flat surface.
2. Make a padding "sausage" by crumpling and rolling tissue or wrapping polyester batting in prepared fabric.
3. Prepare three-dimensional textiles for folding by padding

each seam with a "sausage" to prevent compression; sleeves, pant legs, and folded collars should also be padded.

4. Fold sleeves or other extensions inward, padding the fold with a "sausage."
5. Using the box length, decide how many folds will be required to make the textile fit snugly but without being crumpled or forced to fit. Try to fold a textile the least number of times possible to make it fit into the box; every fold causes tension on the textile.
7. After folding the textile, wrap it with cotton, muslin, or tissue and place it into an acid-free box.

APPENDIX 14

Making Padding for Ceramic and Glass Storage

Materials and Supply List

- lightweight canvas, muslin, or cotton fabric (fabric should be washed and unbleached)
- poly-pellets (can be purchased at most crafts stores)
- lead shot (if using shot supports, should be double bagged in fabric to prevent the powder of the shot from penetrating the fabric)
- ethafoam or polyethylene foam to make forms (may be purchased in many shapes or in blocks)
- thread (100 percent cotton or cotton/polyester blend)
- needle
- scissors
- sewing machine

1. Cut the fabric into the shape and size required to adequately support the artifact. When supporting an object from underneath the support "pillow" should extend slightly beyond the bottom edge of the artifact when filled with poly-pellets or shot. If the support is to wrap around the

Diagram 34

Flexible shapes or tubes that may be wrapped around the base of an object

Support "pillows" of any shape to offer the support needed

Examples of different support shapes for Glass and Ceramics

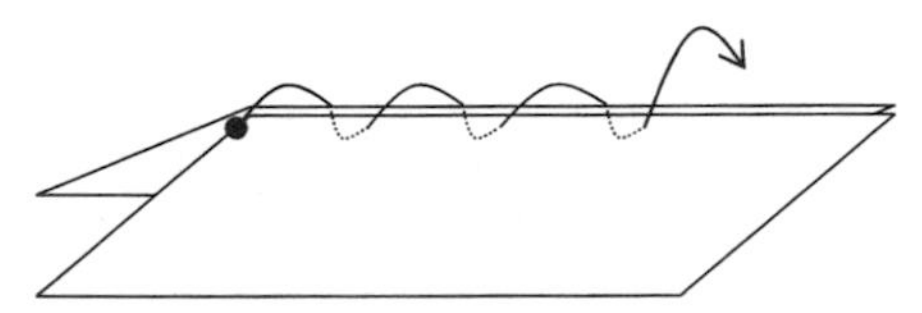

Hand whipstitch — for joining seams of filled supports

With the fabrics to be joined held close together, starting at the inside fold (seam allowance) of the fabric. The thread passes "runs" over the folded edges of both fabrics, then passes though both fabrics slightly below the fold. When the seam is pulled together, the thread is visible and there is a slight ridge

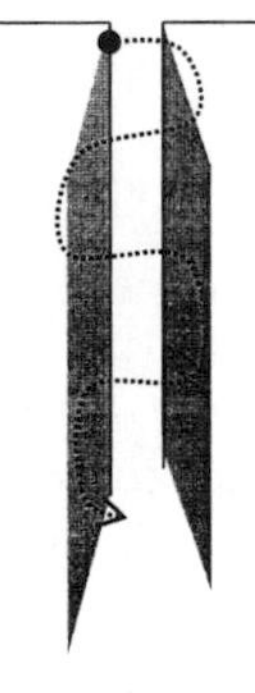

Starting at the inside fold of the fabric, the thread is passed through both fabrics then "runs" in the fold of the opposite fabric. When the seam is pulled together, no thread is visible

Hand blind stitch — for joining seams of filled supports

Diagram 35

bottom of the artifact, like a doughnut shape to prevent tipping, the support should fit exactly to the dimension of the object.

2. Sew the fabric into shape leaving one edge open.
3. Invert the shape so seams are inside the fabric form.
4. Fill the fabric form with poly-pellets or shot. If using lead shot, it should be placed inside a cloth bag prior to being placed in the fabric support form.
5. Hand stitch the final open edge using a blind stitch or a whipstitch over the turned edges of the fabric.

APPENDIX 15

Some Materials for Preservation by Artifact Type

Definitions of most materials can be found in the glossary.

The Basic Tool Box

- pencils
- straight edge
- measuring tape or ruler
- cutting mat (optional)
- utility knife or other cutting blade
- bone folder (optional)
- scissors
- compressed air or air bulb
- vacuum
- drafting brush or
- soft natural bristle dusting brush
- lint free dusting cloths
- weights (can be home-made, see Appendix 14)
- gloves: cotton, nylon, nitrile, latex, polyvinyl, or sure-grip (depending on the type of artifacts in your collection)
- humidity cards, gauge, or thermohygrometer

Other

- milenex or other polyester laminate
- 3M Scotch brand #415 double sided tape
- clean white sheets or washed muslin
- polyethylene sheets, rolls, or bags

Support Boards

- coroplast
- foam core
- acid-free matt board
- acid-free cardboard

Tissues and Papers

- glassine
- permalife
- phototex
- acid-free tissue
- acid-free buffered tissue
- Tyvek

Materials: Books and Paper

- document cleaning pads (do not use coarser types of ground erasers)
- gum erasers
- vinyl erasers
- linen tape
- Melinex or other polyester laminate
- polyvinyl acetate — PVA

Materials: Textiles

- acid-free cardboard
- acid-free storage tubes
- cotton thread
- un-dyed cotton ribbon
- muslin
- polyester batting
- polyester screening
- polyethylene bags
- twill tape
- 3M Scotch brand #415 double sided tape

Materials: Ceramics and Glass

- ethafoam
- museum mounting wax
- clear museum gel
- support bags (see Appendix 14)

Products to Never Use Near Artifacts

- Brown cardboard boxes — acidic
- Office paper — acidic
- Polyurethane foam- acidic, off gases, deteriorates (yellow toned foam often used for making mattresses etc. as it deteriorates leaves a sticky residue
- Rubber bands
- Paper clips or other metal clasps
- Wool felt — attracts insects
- Polyvinyl chloride (PVC)

GLOSSARY

Accession List A record of all holdings, often including a control or reference number and additional information.

Acid A chemical compound that forms from hydrogen (H^+) ions when they are dissolved in water. Acid compounds have a pH less than 7.0. Acids can weaken many artifacts and lead to deterioration.

Acid-free There are several standards for paper to be considered acid-free. Some consider any paper having a pH of 6.8 to 7.0 to be acid-free. Acid-free paper products are produced from cotton fibres, rags, jute, chemical wood pulps, or virtually any other fibre, with precautions taken during fabrication to eliminate any active acid that might be present in the pulp. However free of acid, the paper can be contaminated immediately after manufacture by the presence of residual chlorine from bleaching, aluminum sulfate (alum) from sizing, or sulfur dioxide in the atmosphere that leads to the formation of acids, unless the paper has been **buffered**.

Acid Migration The transfer of acid from an acidic material to a less acidic or pH neutral material through contact.

Alkaline Alkali compounds are considered bases and have a pH greater than 7.0. Alkali materials can be added to a material to neutralize acid or as "buffer" creating an alkali reserve.

Auxiliary Support A board or other support structure that is not part of the artifact but is used to support or strengthen the artifact during handling, display, or storage.

Binding (Bound) The method used to assemble a series of folios and signatures to form a book. Bindings can be sewn, glued, or secured using other forms of hardware.

Book Block The text block of a book plus any additions, such as end sheets, that are added in the binding process.

Buckling A distortion from plane resulting in warping, bulging, or undulations of what should be a flat planar support. Buckling can be random or localized in affected areas.

Buffering Refers to a compound that reacts with any added acid to control the pH. The preferred buffering agent for preservation is calcium carbonate.

Cellulose The fibres formed in the cell wall of green plants. Cellulose is a component of many products including paper and textiles.

Conservation Consists of the examination, stabilization, reconstruction, and environmental assessment of an object. Conservation often involves scientific analysis of the object and the materials used in fabrication, research into the structure and historic significance, and determination of condition, stability, and losses. Conservation also includes the structural and chemical stabilization and environmental treatment to slow the deterioration of an object.

Coroplast® A rigid corrugated copolymer of 90 percent polypropylene and 10 percent polyethylene. It is considered to be chemically stable, is resistant to heat, and does not absorb grease, oil, or acids.

Crizzling (glass) A form of glass deterioration related to incorrect formulation during fabrication that appears like a fine series of cracks.

Deacidification A chemical treatment that neutralizes acid in a material, such as paper, and deposits an alkali buffer to reduce future acid accumulation. This treatment is sometimes referred to by conservators as "neutralization and alkalization." This process does not restore strength or repair damage but it does increase chemical stability and can reduce the rate of further deterioration.

Desiccation Describes the process of moisture release and drying. Literally means to dry out thoroughly. This term is often used when referring to paper, adhesives, and woods.

Deformation A change in shape or size due to an applied force. This term is often used in conservation to refer to objects that are no longer flat or square due to exposure to high levels of humidity or moisture.

Document Cleaning Pads Fine eraser powder enclosed in a fabric bag. Used to clean surfaces, not recommended for cleaning pencil, pastel, or other loose medium artifacts.

Double Sided Tape 3M 415 A double sided tape with a carrier strip that should never be used in direct contact with an artifact.

Drafting Brush or **Dusting Brushes** A traditional architect's tool, these long and narrow brushes are used to brush away eraser residue and for dusting. The bristles are usually a single row of tufts, often sterilized horse hair, that run about three-quarters of the length of the brush from the tip to the handle.

Efflorescence Soluble salts and other water dispersible materials deposited onto the surface of an artifact. Low temperatures, moist conditions, condensation, or exposure to water all promote formation of salt crystals. Efforescence can occur very soon after exposure to moist or cool conditions, or gradually.

Encapsulate To enclose or encase within a protective container, usually polyester laminate or film (Melinex) that has been sealed on all sides. The artifact is not adhered to the plastic and can be easily removed by opening one edge.

End Sheet or **End Papers** The proper term is end paper but end sheet is commonly used. These terms refer to the blank fly leaves of a book.

Fibre A natural or synthetic filament typically capable of being spun into thread or yarn.

Filament Often used to refer to synthetic fibres that are extruded in long thread-like structures, but can refer to natural fibre threads as well.

Foam Core Be sure to buy white, acid-free board, not the presentation board offered at office supply stores. Used for auxiliary support when handling unframed works of art, for box construction, and as backing boards on paintings.

Foot Candles A unit of measurement for light: 1 foot candle = approximately 11 lux.

Foxing A cause of age-related paper deterioration. Foxing can be a result of the destruction of the **lingin** by sunlight and absorbing atmospheric pollution. It is also attributed to the impurities left within the fibre structure from the manufacturing process. It typically causes brown spotting on the paper.

Frass Wood powder found near the exit holes of insects from wood, basketry, and textiles.

Gesso A material used as a primer on canvas and wood prior to applying paint or gilding. Gesso also generically used to refer to "plaster" that can be carved or moulded to form three-dimensional designs such as on frames.

Gild or **Gilding** A thin layer or gold or other metal.

Glassine A commonly used interleafing and wrapping paper for storage. It is translucent, unbuffered, and acid-free. With time, glassine does absorb acids from the surrounding materials and artifacts and should be changed.

Gum Eraser Used for removing pencil marks and surface soil. Often used in crumb form. Staedtler Gum Eraser Cleaner, for example.

Head Cap The covering at the head and tail (top and bottom) of the spine of a book, formed by turning the covering material on the spine over the head and tail and shaping the spine.

Inert A material that is not easily decomposed or chemically altered.

Infrared Light Light in specific range of wavelengths, like visible light, that range from red light to violet. "Near infrared" light is closest in wavelength to visible light and "far infrared" is closer to the microwave region of the electromagnetic spectrum. Far infrared waves are thermal. We experience this type of infrared radiation every day in the form of heat.

Inherent Vice Forms of deterioration that are directly related to the fabrication or construction of the artifact that cannot be corrected. These vices continue to cause deterioration no matter what precautions are taken.

Interleaf To place sheets of paper, board, tissue, or other appropriate material between two artifacts.

Leaf A sheet of paper forming two pages of the text (front and back).

Lignin Lignin is an integral part of the cell walls of plants. It is a complex chemical compound most commonly derived from wood and found in pulp. Lignin can be removed during the pulping process to produce a higher grade of paper. Because lignin is a cause of chemical deterioration of papers and boards, preservation standards recommend all paper and boards be "lignin-free."

Lumens A unit of measurement for light with the symbol lm. Lumen is a unit of luminous flux, a measure of the perceived power of light. Lumens are related to lux by the following formula: 1 lm = 1 lx·m^2.

Lux The symbol for lux is lx and is the unit of illuminance and luminous emittance. It is used in photometry as a measure of the *apparent* intensity of light hitting or passing through a surface.

Matt The window board that an artifact is viewed through in the mounting package. Matt boards for long term preservation should be 100 percent rag or conservation/museum quality. Boards are either buffered or **unbuffered**. Buffered boards should not be used with animal by-products such as silk, wool, or leather.

Matt burn A darkening where an acidic matt board touches your artifact. The acid from the board is absorbed by your artifact causing deterioration. Often appears as a dark line right at the perimeter of the matt window.

Media/Medium A term used to describe the technique, method or material used by an artist. This can be broken down into the technique where it describes the final product of an artist like painting, drawing, print, etc. These general techniques materials can be subdivided into more specific descriptions of the vehicle or binding agent employed such as acrylic paint, oil pastel, charcoal, encaustic, painting-egg tempera on wood panel, drawing-oil pastel on paper adhered to canvas, etc.

Melinex® (previously known as Mylar) A clear polyester film. It is very stable and available in various thicknesses and formats.

Mil A unit of thickness used of measuring paper and boards. One mil is equal to one thousandth of an inch (0.001″). See **Point**.

Mildew A specific kind of mould or fungus growth, usually related to agriculture, that has a powdery or downy appearance. The term is generically used to refer to mould growth that has a flat profile.

Mordant A chemical that fixes a dye on a base such as thread or cloth. A mordant combines with the dye to form an insoluble compound.

Mould The growth of microscopic fungi. Mould can thrive on any organic matter, including clothing, leather, paper, and the ceilings, walls, and floors of homes with moisture management problems. There are many species of mould. In un-aired places, such as basements, they can produce a strong musty odour.

Mount A solid piece of matt board or other appropriate board used to support an artifact either in storage or display.

Paper Made from the extracted cellulose material of wood pulp. Also generically used to refer to skins of an animal, better identified by the terms parchment or vellum.

Parchment The untanned skin of an animal (usually sheep, calf, or goat) that is prepared for writing or drawing. Parchment has been used for millenia. Often diplomas were referred to as parchments as they were traditionally written on this support.

Patina A layer of metal oxidation on the surface of an artifact. This layer protects the metal and can be applied intentionally by an artist or manufacturer. Most patinas should not be removed without consultation with a conservator as removal can lower the value of the artifact.

Permalife A paper developed by Dr. W. J. Barrow to exceed standards for durability and permanence. In simulated testing for usage equalling more than 300 years, it neither yellowed nor became brittle. It is buffered with a pH value of 7.5 to 8.0.

pH The measure of the concentration of hydrogen (H^+) ions on a scale from 0 to 14. Each number represents a tenfold increase in the number of ions.

pH 7 is neutral
below 7= acidic with 1 being the most acidic
above 7 = alkaline with 14 being the most alkali
Paper with a pH below 5 is considered to be highly acidic.

Photo Activity Test (PAT) A globally recognized standard developed by the Image Permanence Institute (IPI) to determine the archival quality of photo-storage products.

Phototex Unbuffered, lightweight, 100 percent rag interleafing paper for photos and wrapping of textiles.

Point A unit of thickness used of measuring paper and boards. One point is equal to one thousandth of an inch (0.001″) see **Mil**.

Polish An abrasive substance used to remove tarnish and some surface metal.

Polyester A chemically stable material used to produce products such as cloth, batting (stuffing), and film sheets such as Melinex.

Polyethylene A very flexible plastic that may be used for storage of artifacts.

Polypropylene A chemically stable plastic used for storage.

Polyvinyl chloride (PVC) As PVC deteriorates with age, hydrochloric acid, which damages artifacts, is emitted. PVC has been used in an assortment of products including enclosures for slides and negatives, coin holders, and sheet protectors for documents.

Preservation A small part of the conservation process that focuses on treatments to retard further deterioration of an object caused by environmental influences.

Primer A product applied to the support material to prepare the surface for painting. Numerous materials can be used to make primers and they can be any colour. They usually improve the adhesion of the paint to the support.

Protein Loosely used to describe products derived from animals such as wool, silk, or hair.

Relative Humidity The amount of water vapour in the air at any given time is usually less than that required to saturate the air. The relative humidity is the percent of saturation humidity, generally calculated in relation to saturated vapour density.

$$\text{Relative Humidity} = \frac{\text{actual vapour density}}{\text{saturation vapour density}} \times 100\%$$

Restoration A small part of the conservation process that reconstructs the aesthetic appearance of an object.

Reversibility The ability to undo a process or treatment with no change to the artifact. It is an ideal for all conservation procedures and is virtually impossible to attain but dictates the balance of all options available for the long-term stability of the object.

Selvadge (Selvege) The edge on either side of a flat woven fabric formed by the weft threads. This edge often appears as a narrow border composed of heavier threads and sometimes has a different weave pattern.

Signature (book) All the leaves of a book or pamphlet formed by folding a single sheet of paper.

Size (Sizing) Often a glue or gum substance applied to paper or fabric. Sizing is used on fibres during manufacture in order to retard their tendency to absorb liquids.

Solandar Boxes Named for their inventor Daniel Solander, these are made from sturdy pressboard or binder's board. Many are manufactured today using buffered, acid-free board, or other neutral materials as the lining of the box.

Spine The backbone of a book. This is where a book is bound and is the portion of a book that you see when the book is shelved.

Strainer A frame over which the support fabric or material is stretched taut. Strainers do not have expandable corners. As a painting ages, it slackens on a strainer.

Stretcher A frame over which the support fabric or materials is stretched taut. Stretchers have expandable corners so the tension can be adjusted.

Support The material to which the media are applied in the production of art and artifacts; for example: paper, wood, or vellum.

Synthetic An artificial fibre or compound.

Text block The body of a book made up of the leaves or signatures.

Textile A cloth or construction made from fibres, filaments, or yarns; often woven or knitted.

Tide Lines Caused when soluble salts and other water-dispersible materials are wicked into the structure of an artifact and then they dry. The result is a line of salt and contaminates deposited along the line where water stopped travelling through the structure.

Tissue

> **Acid-free Tissue** Used for wrapping protein-based artifacts (wool, leather, hair, silk, etc.), mixed media artifacts such as costumes, padding when boxing textiles, and interleafing for albums, prints, and contemporary colour photographs.
>
> **Acid-free Buffered Tissue** Used for wrapping cellulose-based artifacts (cotton, linen, paper, etc.) and for interleafing.

Tyvek® A smooth, non-woven, fibre-spun Olefin that is inert and gas permeable. It is resistant to micro-organism growth, tearing, water, and dust. It can be sewn, taped, or heat sealed. It is used for making enclosures for textiles, protective covers, labels, envelopes, and much more.

Ultraviolet Scientists have divided the ultraviolet part of the spectrum into three regions: the near ultraviolet, the far ultraviolet, and the extreme ultraviolet. The three regions are distinguished by how energetic the ultraviolet radiation is and by the "wavelength" of the ultraviolet light, which is related to energy. Most people are aware of the effects of UV through the painful condition of sunburn, but the UV spectrum has many other effects, both beneficial and damaging.

Unbuffered In paper products, no buffering agents, such as calcium carbonate, have been applied during fabrication to help resist acid penetration and build-up.

Vinyl Erasers Soft, easy to cut for a clean edge, general purpose erasers (Magic Gum®, Staedtler Mars Plastic).

Warp The yarns that are extended lengthwise on a loom to form the base of a fabric.

Weep (glass) A form of glass deterioration related to incorrect formulation during fabrication. It appears like droplets or dampness on the glass surface. It is highly alkaline.

Weft (Woof) The yarns used to fill in the warp. These yarns run perpendicular to the loom and form the selvage edge.

Vellum A fine-grained lamb, kid, or calfskin prepared for writing or binding books. In the Middle Ages, the skin of an unborn calf was used.

REFERENCE AND FURTHER READING

Canadian Conservation Institute-Institut Canadien de Conservation. *CCI Notes- Notes de I'ICC.* Ottawa: Canadian Conservation Institute-Institut Canadien de Conservation (CCI-l'ICC), 1992.

Douglas, Althea. *Help! I've Inherited an Attic Full of History.* Toronto: Ontario Genealogical Society, 2003.

Dudley, Dorothy H, Irma Bezold Wilkinson, et al. *Museum Registration Methods.* Washington, D.C: American Association of Museums, 1979.

Ellis, Margaret Holben. *The Care of Prints and Drawings.* Nashville, Tennessee: American Associations for State and Local History Press, 1987.

Gaylord Bros. *Gaylord Preservation Pathfinder No. 1: Introduction to Preservation.* Syracuse, New York: Gaylord Bros., 1993

———— . *Gaylord Preservation Pathfinder No. 2: Archival Storage of Paper.* Syracuse, New York: Gaylord Bros., 1993.

Greenfield, Jane. *Books Their Care & Repair.* New York: The H. Wilson Company, 1983.

Hanna, Janette and Burge, Daniel. "Preserving Digital Memory Files." *Image Permanence Institute www.archivaladvisor.org/shtml/art_presdigmem.shtml* (accessed 20 May 2009)

Keefe, L. and Inch, D. *Life of a Photograph: Archival Processing, Matting, Framing and Storage* 2nd ed. Focal Press, Boston, MA, 1990.

Schultz, Arthur W. ed. *Caring for your Collections.* New York: Harry N. Abrams Inc. Publishers, 1992.

Schwalberg, B., Wilheim, H., and Bower, C. "Going! Going!! Gone!!!" *Popular Photography.* June 1990, 37–49, 60.

Story, Keith O. *Approaches to Pest Management in Museums.* Washington, DC: Smithsonian Institution, 1985.

U.S. Library of Congress *Preserving your Digital Memories www.digital-preservation.gov/you/digitalmemories.html* (accessed 14 July 2009).

Wilson, Colleen. *Tales from the Attic. Practical Advice on Preserving Heirlooms and Collectibles.* Victoria: Royal British Columbia Museum, 2002.

Zeier, Franz. *Books, Boxes and Portfolios: Binding, Construction and Design Step-by-Step.* New York: Design Press, 1983.

SUPPLIERS

Many materials and supplies may be purchased at local craft, art, and hardware stores.

Archival Products
2957 Inlake Court
Mississauga, ON L5N 2A4
(905) 858-7888
1-800-667-2632
info@archivalproducts.ca
www.archivalproducts.ca

Canadian Representative of Gaylord Bros.
Canadian Representative of University Products
Carr McLean
461 Horner Ave.
Toronto, On M8W 4X4
1-800-268-2123
www.carrmclean.ca

Suppliers

Gaylord Bros., Inc.
P.O. Box 4901
Syracuse, NY 13221-4901
1-800-634-6307
customerservice@gaylord.com
www.gaylord.com

Light Impressions
P.O. Box 2100
Santa Fe Springs, CA 90670
1-800-828-6216
www.LightImpressionsDirect.com

University Products
517 Main Street
P.O. Box 101
Holyoke, MA 01041-0101
1-800-628-1912
www.universityproducts.com

Other Genealogist's Reference Shelf Titles

GENEALOGICAL STANDARDS OF EVIDENCE

A Guide for Family Historians

Brenda Dougall Merriman

978-1-55488-451-3

Genealogy and family history revolve around issues of identification. Genealogical evidence is the information — analyzed and evaluated — that allows us to identify an individual, an event in his or her life, or the relationship between individuals. This book will tell you about how the genealogical community developed standards of evidence and documentation, what those standards are, and how you can apply them to your own work.

GENEALOGY AND THE LAW IN CANADA

Dr. Margaret Ann Wilkinson

978-1-55488-452-0

The development of digital records and broad access to the web has revolutionized the ways in which genealogists approach their investigations — and has made it much easier to locate relevant information. The law, on the other hand, remains very connected to particular geographic locations. This book discusses the relevant laws — access to information, protection of personal data, and copyright — applicable to those working within Canada with materials that are located in Canada.